Sentinels of the Digital Realm

Mastering Cyber Defense

Dinesh Kumar

Preface

In today's interconnected world, cyber threats evolve at lightning speed. Cybersecurity is no longer just a technical challenge—it's essential for protecting our digital lives. **"Sentinels of the Digital Realm: Mastering Cyber Defense"** is designed to empower you to become a vigilant guardian of your organization's digital assets, equipping you with practical strategies to build a resilient defense.

Over the past decades, cyber-attacks have evolved from simple viruses into sophisticated intrusions targeting critical infrastructures and sensitive data. As our reliance on digital technology grows, so does our exposure to risk. This book offers a comprehensive yet practical framework for cyber defense, blending foundational principles with advanced strategies essential for today's dynamic threat landscape.

Structure and Approach

The book is organized into parts that together form a robust defense framework:

- **Foundations of Cyber Defense:**
  Explore core principles like the CIA triad, risk management, and defense in depth.

- **Core Pillars of Cyber Defense:**
  Delve into network security, endpoint protection, identity and access management (IAM), and data protection with real-world case studies and actionable tasks.

- **Advanced Topics and Emerging Trends:**
  Discover cutting-edge areas such as offensive security,

cyber threat intelligence, AI and machine learning, quantum computing, and IoT/OT security.

- **Governance, Compliance, and Strategy:** Address the strategic, regulatory, and organizational aspects of cybersecurity, from global cyber laws to building a successful career.

Why "Sentinels of the Digital Realm"?

The title reflects the vital role of cybersecurity professionals as vigilant guardians in the vast digital landscape. As "sentinels," you are entrusted with protecting every byte of data and ensuring the integrity of your organization's digital environment. "Mastering Cyber Defense" signals that this book provides advanced insights and practical guidance to help you stay ahead of emerging threats.

My journey in cybersecurity has taught me that effective defense requires both technical skill and continuous learning. It's about integrating cutting-edge technology with strategic thinking, risk management, and a culture of security. This book encapsulates that holistic approach—combining theory with actionable steps to empower you in securing your digital realm.

Looking Ahead

I encourage you to engage deeply with the material—perform the exercises, reflect on the case studies, and adapt the concepts to your unique environment. Cybersecurity is ever evolving, and the insights provided here will serve as a foundation for your ongoing professional growth.

— Dinesh Kumar

Contents

Part 1: Foundations of Cyber Defense

Chapter 1: Introduction to Cybersecurity

Cybersecurity touches nearly every aspect of modern life. It protects personal information, secures financial transactions, and safeguards the critical systems that power our society. This book focuses specifically on **Cyber Defense**—the proactive measures taken to protect digital assets and respond effectively to attacks. In this chapter, we introduce the fundamentals of cybersecurity, explore the evolution of cyber threats with modern examples and data, and provide real-world case studies along with actionable steps. Our goal is to lay a solid foundation for your journey into the world of cyber defense.

1.1 What Is Cybersecurity?

Cybersecurity is the practice of protecting computers, networks, programs, and data from unauthorized access, damage, or disruption. Think of it as a comprehensive security system for your digital life. Just as a home security system uses locks, alarms, and cameras to deter intruders, cybersecurity employs a mix of technologies, policies, and best practices to fend off digital threats.

Rather than relying on a single tool, effective cybersecurity builds layers of defense. If one layer fails, another stands ready to minimize risk. This layered approach is at the heart of cyber defense strategies discussed throughout this book.

Expert Insight

Bruce Schneier once said, "Security is a process, not a product." Continuous improvement is essential in cybersecurity.

1.2 The Evolution of Cyber Threats

Early Viruses to Advanced Persistent Threats

In the early days of computing, viruses were simple programs that spread by replicating themselves across systems. These early threats were more of a nuisance than a critical concern.

Today's cyber-attacks, however, are far more sophisticated. Modern threats like Advanced Persistent Threats (APTs) infiltrate networks slowly, remain undetected for long periods, and exfiltrate sensitive data. Such attacks are often executed by organized groups—including nation-states—and target high-value assets.

Real-World Example: WannaCry Ransomware

The WannaCry ransomware attack in 2017 is a stark example of modern cyber threats. WannaCry exploited a vulnerability in outdated Windows systems and spread rapidly affecting over **200,000 computers worldwide**. Once a system was infected, the ransomware encrypted files and demanded a Bitcoin payment for decryption.

How WannaCry Unfolded:

- **Propagation:** Using an exploit called EternalBlue, WannaCry moved quickly through unpatched systems.

- **Impact:** Critical services, such as hospitals, suffered severe disruptions; patient records became inaccessible, putting lives at risk.

- **Consequences:** Beyond financial losses, WannaCry exposed the dangers of neglecting timely software updates and robust network segmentation.

- **Lessons Learned:** Regular patch management, thorough vulnerability assessments, and layered defenses are essential.

Real-World Example: The Equifax Data Breach

In 2017, the Equifax breach compromised the personal data of nearly 150 million individuals. Attackers exploited an unpatched vulnerability in a web application framework, gaining access to sensitive records like Social Security numbers and birth dates.

How the Breach Unfolded:

- **Exploitation:** A failure to update software allowed attackers to bypass security controls.

- **Impact:** The breach not only caused massive financial and legal repercussions but also eroded consumer trust in data privacy practices.

- **Lessons Learned:** Continuous vulnerability assessments and proactive risk management are critical to protecting sensitive data.

Modern Threats: Recent Examples

Recent incidents, such as the 2023 MOVEit data theft and the Colonial Pipeline ransomware attack, further highlight that cyber threats continue to evolve. These examples underscore the importance of keeping defenses up to date as attackers refine their techniques.

1.3 Key Concepts in Cybersecurity

The CIA Triad: Confidentiality, Integrity, and Availability

The CIA triad is a foundational model in cybersecurity:

- **Confidentiality:** Ensures that sensitive information is accessed only by those who are authorized—like keeping your personal diary private.

- **Integrity:** Maintains the accuracy and trustworthiness of data, ensuring that records such as bank statements reflect true values.

- **Availability:** Guarantees that data and systems are accessible when needed, such as an e-commerce site remaining operational during peak times.

A breach in any of these areas can lead to significant disruptions, from data leaks to service outages.

Defense in Depth

Defense in depth involves multiple layers of security controls. Imagine a medieval castle with multiple walls and moats—if an attacker breaches the outer wall, additional defenses still protect the core.

In practice, this might include:

- **Firewalls** to filter network traffic,

- **Intrusion Detection Systems (IDS)** to flag suspicious activity,

- **Antivirus software** to remove malware,

- **Strict access controls** to limit who can reach sensitive data.

Technical Teaser:
A firewall, for example, can be thought of as a filter that examines every data packet. Simple packet filtering checks basic information (like IP addresses), while stateful firewalls track active connections to determine if incoming data is part of an established conversation. Next-Generation Firewalls (NGFW) go further by analyzing the content of data packets to detect potential threats.

1.4 The Human Element in Cybersecurity

Even the most advanced technical systems can be undermined by human error. Cyber-attacks often exploit human vulnerabilities through social engineering.

Social Engineering and Phishing

Phishing emails are a common tactic. These messages are designed to look like they come from trusted sources—such as your bank or a popular online service—and trick you into revealing sensitive information.

Step-by-Step Breakdown of a Phishing Email:

1. **Sender Address:** The email may appear to come from a legitimate source but often contains subtle errors.

2. **Urgent Language:** A sense of urgency is created (e.g., "Your account will be suspended!").

3. **Suspicious Links:** Hovering over links reveals mismatched or unusual URLs.

4. **Unexpected Attachments:** The email might include attachments you weren't expecting.

Regular training and awareness can help you recognize and avoid these scams.

1.5 Cybersecurity in the Real World

Cybersecurity is not just a technical concept—it directly affects your daily life and critical societal functions.

Protecting Personal Data

Every online transaction—from banking to social media—involves the handling of personal data. Using strong passwords, multi-factor authentication, and secure networks is essential for keeping your information safe.

Safeguarding Businesses and Critical Infrastructure

Organizations rely on secure digital systems for daily operations. Cyber-attacks can disrupt business operations, lead to financial losses, and damage reputations. Moreover, critical infrastructure—such as power grids, transportation systems, and water treatment facilities—depends on cybersecurity to protect public safety.

Statistic: According to recent reports, the cybersecurity job market is projected to grow by approximately 31% by 2029, reflecting the increasing demand for skilled professionals.

1.6 Everyday Cyber Hygiene

Developing good cyber hygiene habits is the first step toward protecting yourself online. Here are some practical measures you can start with today:

1. **Use Strong Passwords:**
   Create complex passwords with a mix of letters, numbers, and symbols. A password manager can help generate and store unique passwords.

2. **Keep Software Updated:**
   Regular updates include critical security patches that protect against known vulnerabilities.

3. **Exercise Caution with Emails:**
   Verify the sender's address and be wary of unsolicited links or attachments.

4. **Regular Backups:**
   Back up important data using cloud services or external drives to mitigate data loss.

5. **Secure Your Home Network:**
   Use strong Wi-Fi passwords and consider creating a guest network for visitors.

Actionable Task

Before moving on, take a moment to:

- **Audit Your Passwords:** Update any weak or reused passwords.

- **Review Software Updates:** Ensure all your devices are running the latest versions.

- **Examine Your Inbox:** Identify and report any suspicious emails.

These simple steps lay the foundation for a secure digital life.

1.7 The Technological Landscape of Cyber Defense

Modern cybersecurity relies on a variety of specialized tools. Here's a brief overview:

- **Firewalls:** Act as gatekeepers that filter incoming and outgoing network traffic.

- **Encryption:** Secures data by converting it into a coded format. For instance, AES (Advanced Encryption Standard) is preferred for its strong protection against brute-force attacks.

- **Intrusion Detection/Prevention Systems (IDS/IPS):** Monitor network traffic to detect and block potential threats.

- **SIEM Systems:** Collect and analyze data from various sources to identify anomalies in real time.

Note: Detailed technical explorations of these tools will be provided in later chapters.

1.8 Cybersecurity Careers: An Emerging Frontier

The growing complexity of cyber threats has opened up numerous career opportunities in cyber defense. Whether you're interested in technical roles or strategic positions, there's a path for you.

Diverse Roles in Cyber Defense

- **Security Operations Center (SOC) Analyst:**
  Monitors network traffic and responds to security incidents.
  Key Skills: Analytical thinking, SIEM tools, network protocols.

- **Penetration Tester (Ethical Hacker):**
  Simulates attacks to identify vulnerabilities before they are exploited.
  Key Skills: Programming, creative problem-solving, network security.

- **Threat Intelligence Analyst:**
  Analyzes cyber threat patterns and predicts future attacks.
  Key Skills: Research, data analysis, OSINT.

- **Digital Forensics Expert:**
  Investigates cyber-crimes and preserves digital evidence.
  Key Skills: Detail orientation, forensic tools, legal knowledge.

- **Cybersecurity Consultant:**
  Advises organizations on implementing robust cybersecurity strategies.
  Key Skills: Broad technical knowledge, regulatory awareness, strategic planning.

Resources for Aspiring Cyber Defenders

For those interested in exploring these careers further, consider:

- **Online Courses:** Platforms like TryHackMe, Cybrary, and Coursera offer hands-on training.

- **Books:** "Cybersecurity for Dummies" and "The Art of Invisibility" provide accessible introductions.

- **Certifications:** CISSP, CEH, OSCP, and CompTIA Security+ are highly regarded in the industry.

- **Professional Organizations:** Join communities such as $(ISC)^2$ and CompTIA for networking and learning opportunities.

1.9 The Future of Cybersecurity

The cybersecurity landscape is dynamic and ever-changing. New technologies and evolving threats mean that defenders must continuously adapt.

- **AI & Machine Learning:** Enhance threat detection by rapidly analyzing vast data sets, though attackers are also leveraging these tools.

- **Quantum Computing:** Promises revolutionary advancements but poses challenges to traditional encryption methods, prompting research into quantum-resistant algorithms.

- **IoT & Critical Infrastructure:** The growing number of connected devices increases the attack surface, making robust defenses more crucial than ever.

Staying informed and continuously updating your skills is vital in this fast-paced field.

Chapter Takeaways

Key Points:

- **Cybersecurity** is the practice of protecting digital assets from unauthorized access and disruptions.

- The **evolution of cyber threats** has moved from simple viruses to sophisticated attacks such as APTs, as seen in incidents like WannaCry and Equifax.

- Foundational concepts like the **CIA triad** (Confidentiality, Integrity, Availability) and **defense in depth** are critical for effective cyber defense.

- **Everyday cyber hygiene**—including strong passwords, regular updates, and cautious email practices—is essential for personal security.

- The technological landscape includes **firewalls, encryption, IDS/IPS,** and **SIEM systems**, all of which will be explored in greater depth later.

- A variety of **career paths** exist in cybersecurity, and continuous learning is key to staying ahead in this evolving field.

Test Your Knowledge

1. **Which element of the CIA triad is compromised when sensitive information is exposed?**
   A. Confidentiality
   B. Integrity
   C. Availability

2. **What does defense in depth mean in a cybersecurity context?**
   A. Using one robust security tool
   B. Implementing multiple layers of security controls
   C. Relying solely on software updates

3. **Name one lesson learned from the WannaCry ransomware attack.**

Final Thoughts

Cybersecurity is a dynamic, ever-evolving field that requires continuous learning and proactive defense strategies. This chapter has provided a solid foundation, covering essential concepts, real-world case studies, and practical steps for everyday security. Reflect on your digital habits, complete the actionable tasks, and use the quiz to test your understanding.

As you progress through this book, you will explore detailed frameworks and techniques that form the backbone of effective cyber defense. Your journey into cybersecurity starts here—with the knowledge and tools to build a resilient digital future.

Thank you for joining us in this introductory chapter. Your path to mastering cyber defense begins now.

End of Chapter 1

Cybersecurity frameworks and standards serve as blueprints for building a robust defense against cyber threats. They offer structured guidelines, best practices, and benchmarks that organizations can use to assess, implement, and continually improve their security posture. In this chapter, we explore key frameworks and regulatory standards, compare their scopes and complexities, and provide actionable steps for applying them. We also include real-world case studies and practical tasks to help you bridge theory with practice. Building on the fundamentals covered in Chapter 1, this chapter focuses on how these structured approaches translate into effective cyber defense strategies.

2.1 What Are Cybersecurity Frameworks and Standards?

Cybersecurity frameworks are structured sets of guidelines designed to help organizations manage and reduce cybersecurity risk. They provide a common language for describing security practices and offer a roadmap for establishing and maintaining a comprehensive cyber defense program. Standards, on the other hand, often carry regulatory weight by defining mandatory requirements to protect sensitive data and ensure compliance with legal obligations.

Frameworks and standards not only outline technical controls but also address administrative policies and procedures. They serve as critical tools for ensuring consistency and reliability in cyber defense practices across different industries and organizations.

Glossary Note:
SIEM: Security Information and Event Management – a technology that aggregates and analyzes activity from various resources to detect threats.

2.2 Key Cybersecurity Frameworks

NIST Cybersecurity Framework

The NIST Cybersecurity Framework is widely adopted in the United States and is built around five core functions:

- **Identify:** Understand organizational assets and risks.

- **Protect:** Implement safeguards to secure critical infrastructure.

- **Detect:** Develop activities to identify cybersecurity events.

- **Respond:** Formulate and execute response strategies.

- **Recover:** Plan for restoring capabilities after incidents.

Comparison Insight:
NIST is versatile and detailed, making it suitable for organizations of various sizes, whereas ISO/IEC 27001 offers a more formalized management system structure.

ISO/IEC 27001

ISO/IEC 27001 is an international standard that specifies the requirements for establishing, implementing, maintaining, and continually improving an Information Security Management System (ISMS). It focuses on:

- Systematically managing sensitive information.

- Implementing risk assessments and treatment plans.

- Ensuring business continuity and compliance with legal requirements.

Organizations that achieve ISO 27001 certification demonstrate a high commitment to security, which can build trust among clients and partners.

CIS Controls

The Center for Internet Security (CIS) Controls comprise a set of prioritized actions to protect against the most pervasive cyber-attacks. They emphasize:

- Inventory and control of hardware and software.

- Continuous vulnerability management.

- Secure configuration of systems.

- Proactive defense measures.

The CIS Controls are highly actionable and provide specific steps that organizations can take to quickly improve their security posture.

MITRE ATT&CK Framework

Unlike the other frameworks, MITRE ATT&CK is a knowledge base of adversary tactics, techniques, and procedures (TTPs) based on real-world observations. It helps security teams to:

- Map and analyze attacker behavior.

- Identify gaps in existing defenses.

- Enhance threat detection and response strategies.

While not a compliance standard, MITRE ATT&CK is invaluable for guiding threat hunting and proactive defense initiatives.

2.3 Regulatory Standards

In addition to voluntary frameworks, organizations must comply with various regulatory standards that impose mandatory security requirements.

General Data Protection Regulation (GDPR)

- **Scope:** Applies to any organization that processes the personal data of EU citizens.

- **Focus:** Protecting individual privacy and giving data subjects greater control over their information.

- **Key Requirements:**

  - **Right to be Forgotten:** Individuals can request the deletion of their data.

  - **Breach Notification:** Mandatory reporting within 72 hours of a breach.

  - **Penalties:** Fines up to 4% of annual global turnover for non-compliance.

Health Insurance Portability and Accountability Act (HIPAA)

- **Scope:** Governs healthcare providers, health plans, and related entities in the United States.

- **Focus:** Protecting electronic protected health information (ePHI).

- **Key Requirements:**

  - Encryption and secure storage of ePHI.

  - Regular risk assessments and audits.

  - Enforcement actions and fines for breaches.

Payment Card Industry Data Security Standard (PCI-DSS)

- **Scope:** Applies to any organization that handles credit card transactions.

- **Focus:** Safeguarding cardholder data.

- **Key Requirements:**

  - Secure network architecture and strong access controls.

  - Regular monitoring, vulnerability scans, and penetration tests.

  - Strict guidelines for data storage, processing, and transmission.

California Consumer Privacy Act (CCPA)

- **Scope:** Targets businesses operating in California or handling the data of California residents.

- **Focus:** Enhancing consumer privacy rights.

- **Key Requirements:**

  - Transparency in data collection practices.

  - Rights for consumers to access, delete, or opt out of data sharing.

o   Financial penalties for non-compliance.

2.4 Applying Frameworks and Standards

Successfully implementing cybersecurity frameworks and meeting regulatory standards is an ongoing process that involves several critical steps:

Step-by-Step Implementation

1. **Risk Assessment:**
   Identify your organization's critical assets and evaluate potential threats and vulnerabilities. This helps you prioritize where to focus your security efforts.

2. **Gap Analysis:**
   Compare your current security posture against the guidelines provided by your chosen framework or standard. Identify deficiencies and areas that need improvement.

3. **Develop an Action Plan:**
   Create a detailed plan that outlines specific measures, timelines, and responsibilities to address identified gaps. This plan should include both technical and administrative controls.

4. **Implement Controls:**
   Deploy the necessary safeguards. For example, if your gap analysis under the NIST framework indicates weak detection capabilities, consider investing in SIEM and IDS/IPS technologies.

5. **Continuous Monitoring and Improvement:**
   Cyber threats evolve constantly, so regularly review
   and update your security measures. Conduct periodic
   audits and adjust your strategies based on new risks
   and emerging technologies.

Interactive Exercise: Framework Selection Checklist

- **Task:** List three critical assets within your organization
  (or personal digital life) and identify potential risks for
  each.

- **Follow-Up:** Select a framework (e.g., NIST or ISO 27001)
  that best aligns with your needs, and note how its core
  functions or controls could address the identified risks.

2.5 Real-World Applications and Case Studies

Understanding frameworks is essential but seeing them in
action can make the concepts tangible.

Case Study 1: Implementing NIST in a Mid-Sized Company

A mid-sized company, following a minor security incident,
decided to adopt the NIST Cybersecurity Framework. Their
journey involved:

- **Identification:** Conducting a thorough inventory of
  assets and a comprehensive risk assessment.

- **Protection:** Implementing multi-factor authentication
  and enhancing firewall configurations.

- **Detection:** Deploying a SIEM system to monitor
  network traffic and flag anomalies.

- **Response:** Establishing a detailed incident response plan with clearly defined roles.

- **Recovery:** Developing a business continuity plan that reduced downtime by 30% after subsequent incidents.

Reflection:

"Had Equifax embraced a similar structured approach, some of the breach's impact might have been mitigated."

Case Study 2: Achieving ISO 27001 Certification in Healthcare

A healthcare provider pursued ISO 27001 certification to strengthen its information security management system (ISMS). Key steps included:

- Establishing an ISMS to manage patient data securely.

- Conducting regular internal audits and risk assessments.

- Implementing strict access controls and data encryption measures.

- Undergoing rigorous external certification audits.

The certification not only improved their security posture but also boosted patient and partner confidence, ultimately resulting in measurable improvements in compliance and incident reduction.

2.6 Comparing Frameworks: A Quick Reference

Below is a simplified comparison of three major frameworks:

Framework/Standard	Focus	Complexity	Industry Applicability
NIST CSF	Risk management & cyber defense	Moderate to High	Government, enterprises, and SMEs
ISO/IEC 27001	Information Security Management	High (formalized ISMS)	Global organizations, especially in regulated industries
CIS Controls	Tactical and operational security	Low to Moderate	SMEs, organizations seeking quick wins

Tip: Use this table as a starting point to determine which framework aligns best with your organization's needs and maturity level.

2.7 Resources and Next Steps

To further your understanding and application of cybersecurity frameworks and standards, consider these resources:

- **Online Courses:**
  - Coursera and Udemy offer courses on NIST and ISO 27001 implementation.

- Cybrary provides hands-on training for CIS Controls and risk management.

- **Books:**

    - *"NIST Cybersecurity Framework: A Pocket Guide"*

    - *"ISO 27001/27002 for the Practitioner"*

- **Professional Organizations:**

    - Join (ISC)^2, ISACA, or CompTIA for networking, training, and certification opportunities.

- **Websites and Blogs:**

    - Follow reputable cybersecurity blogs and news sites for the latest updates and case studies.

Practical Tip: Start small by selecting one framework that aligns with your current needs and gradually expand your security program as you gain experience.

2.8 Chapter Takeaways

Key Points:

- **Frameworks and standards** provide structured guidelines for managing cybersecurity risks and ensuring compliance.

- The **NIST Cybersecurity Framework, ISO/IEC 27001, CIS Controls,** and **MITRE ATT&CK** each offer unique strengths for different organizational needs.

- Regulatory standards like **GDPR, HIPAA, PCI-DSS,** and **CCPA** impose mandatory requirements that enhance data protection.

- A systematic approach—risk assessment, gap analysis, implementation, and continuous improvement—is essential for effective cyber defense.

- Real-world case studies demonstrate the tangible benefits of adopting these structured approaches.

2.9 Test Your Knowledge

1. **Which core function of the NIST Cybersecurity Framework focuses on restoring capabilities after an incident?**
   A. Identify
   B. Protect
   C. Recover
   D. Respond

2. **ISO/IEC 27001 primarily helps organizations to:**
   A. Develop software
   B. Establish an Information Security Management System (ISMS)
   C. Monitor social media
   D. Increase sales

3. **Scenario Question:**
   Imagine you are a security consultant for a mid-sized healthcare organization. Which regulatory standard should you prioritize to protect patient data, and what is one key requirement of that standard?

4. **Framework Reflection:**
   Which cybersecurity framework (NIST, ISO/IEC 27001, or CIS Controls) do you think best aligns with your current needs or organizational goals, and why?

2.10 Final Thoughts

Cybersecurity frameworks and standards are not just theoretical models—they are practical tools that enable organizations to build, measure, and improve their cyber defense strategies. By systematically applying these guidelines, you can transform abstract principles into concrete actions that protect critical assets and enhance overall resilience.

As you continue your journey in this book, you will see how these frameworks integrate with other aspects of cyber defense, such as incident response, cloud security, and threat intelligence. Embrace the structured approach provided by these frameworks and use the exercises and resources in this chapter to start implementing improvements today.

Thank you for exploring Chapter 2. Your understanding of these blueprints for cyber defense is a vital step toward building a more secure digital future.

End of Chapter 2

Risk management is the cornerstone of a resilient cybersecurity program. It transforms uncertainty into actionable insight by identifying potential threats, assessing their impact, and determining strategies to mitigate or accept those risks. In this chapter, we build on the foundational concepts from Chapter 1 and the structured guidelines from Chapter 2, and we dive deep into the "how" of risk management in cyber defense. Through clear explanations, practical exercises, and real-world examples—including global case studies—you'll learn how to systematically manage risks to protect critical assets.

3.1 What Is Risk Management?

Risk management is the systematic process of identifying, evaluating, and mitigating risks to an organization's information assets. It does not aim to eliminate all risk—an impossible task—but to reduce risks to an acceptable level, enabling informed decision-making and resource allocation.

Expert Insight:
"Risk management is about making informed decisions in the face of uncertainty. It is not the avoidance of risk but the intelligent management of it." — Cybersecurity Consultant

By converting uncertainty into actionable data, risk management allows organizations to prioritize their defenses and tailor security measures to emerging threats. This approach is fundamental to effective cyber defense.

3.2 The Risk Management Process

A comprehensive risk management process involves several interrelated stages. Each stage is critical for creating a dynamic defense strategy.

3.2.1 Risk Identification

The first step is to compile an inventory of your critical assets— hardware, software, data, and personnel. During this phase, ask:

- **What are our most valuable assets?**
- **Which threats (cyber-attacks, insider errors, natural disasters) could target these assets?**
- **What vulnerabilities exist in our current systems?**

By identifying these factors, you lay the groundwork for a focused risk assessment.

3.2.2 Risk Assessment

Once risks are identified, they must be evaluated. Risk assessment involves two main components:

- **Qualitative Assessment:** Assigning levels (high, medium, low) based on expert judgment.
- **Quantitative Assessment:** Calculating potential financial impact. For example, **Annualized Loss Expectancy (ALE)** is calculated as:

ALE=Single Loss Expectancy (SLE)×Annual Rate of Occurrence (ARO)\text{ALE} = \text{Single Loss Expectancy (SLE)} \times \text{Annual Rate of Occurrence (ARO)}

Example:

If a data breach is estimated to cost $50,000 each time (SLE) and is expected to occur twice a year (ARO), then:

ALE=50,000×2=$100,000 per year.\text{ALE} = 50,000 \times 2 = \$100,000 \text{ per year.}

A **risk matrix** is often used to plot the likelihood against the impact, enabling easy prioritization of risks.

Visual Note: Imagine a 3×3 grid with "Low," "Medium," and "High" on both axes—a simple risk matrix to guide decision-making.

3.2.3 Risk Mitigation

After assessing risks, determine how to address them. Mitigation strategies typically fall into four categories:

- **Risk Avoidance:** Eliminate activities that expose you to risk (e.g., discontinuing a vulnerable service).

- **Risk Reduction:** Implement controls to lessen the impact or likelihood (e.g., patching software, installing firewalls).

- **Risk Transfer:** Shift risk to a third party, such as through cyber insurance.

- **Risk Acceptance:** When the cost of mitigation exceeds the potential loss, consciously accept the risk.

Quick Reference:
- **Avoidance:** Stop using unsupported software.
- **Reduction:** Regularly update security patches.
- **Transfer:** Use cyber insurance.
- **Acceptance:** Tolerate minor risks with low impact.

3.2.4 Risk Communication

An often-overlooked step is communicating risk to stakeholders. Effective risk communication ensures that decision-makers understand the threats and the rationale behind mitigation efforts. Techniques include:

- **Reporting:** Create clear, concise reports that summarize risk findings, prioritization, and proposed controls.

- **Visual Aids:** Use graphs and risk matrices to illustrate risk levels.

- **Meetings and Workshops:** Present risk assessments in forums where feedback and discussion can refine strategies.

Clear communication builds organizational support and drives timely action.

3.2.5 Risk Monitoring and Review

Risk management is an ongoing process. Regularly monitor your environment to capture new threats and adjust mitigation strategies as needed. Periodic audits, continuous monitoring tools, and updated risk assessments are key to staying ahead of evolving risks.

3.3 Implementing Risk Management in Cyber Defense

A structured risk management plan integrates seamlessly into your overall cybersecurity strategy. Here's a step-by-step guide to implementation:

1. **Establish a Risk Management Policy:**
   Define roles, responsibilities, and assessment criteria. This policy should be aligned with your organization's broader cybersecurity framework.

2. **Conduct a Comprehensive Risk Assessment:**

   - **Asset Inventory:** List your critical digital and physical assets.

   - **Threat and Vulnerability Analysis:** Use tools such as vulnerability scanners and threat intelligence feeds.

   - **Risk Evaluation:** Apply both qualitative and quantitative methods (e.g., risk matrices, ALE calculations).

3. **Develop a Risk Mitigation Plan:**
   Outline specific measures for each risk, including technical, administrative, and physical controls. Prioritize actions based on risk levels.

4. **Implement Controls:**
   Deploy necessary safeguards—firewalls, encryption, multi-factor authentication, and employee training programs.

5. **Communicate Risks:**
   Prepare reports and presentations for stakeholders, ensuring that decision-makers understand the risks and proposed mitigations.

6. **Monitor and Review:**
   Continuously track your risk landscape using

monitoring tools. Update your risk assessments regularly and adjust controls as threats evolve.

Actionable Task

- **Asset Inventory Exercise:**
  Identify your top five critical assets. For each, list one major threat and one vulnerability, and assign a risk level using your risk matrix.

- **Mitigation Plan Development:**
  Choose one identified risk from your inventory and develop a detailed mitigation strategy. Specify which approach (avoidance, reduction, transfer, acceptance) you will use and why.

3.4 Integrating Threat Intelligence

Threat intelligence can significantly enhance your risk management process by providing real-time data on emerging threats. By integrating threat feeds and intelligence reports into your risk assessments, you can:

- **Identify New Threats:** Stay updated on the latest tactics, techniques, and procedures (TTPs) used by attackers.

- **Adjust Risk Priorities:** Modify your risk matrix based on current threat trends.

- **Inform Mitigation Strategies:** Align your defenses with the most relevant and pressing threats.

Personal Note: In my experience, integrating threat intelligence not only sharpened our risk assessments but also helped us preemptively address vulnerabilities that traditional scans missed.

3.5 Real-World Applications and Case Studies

Case Study 1: A Financial Institution's Journey

A mid-sized financial institution overhauled its risk management process after several minor breaches. Their process involved:

- **Risk Identification:** A thorough audit revealed vulnerabilities in legacy software and insufficient employee training.

- **Risk Assessment:** Using both qualitative methods and ALE calculations, they determined that phishing posed a high risk.

- **Risk Mitigation:** They implemented advanced email filtering, conducted regular training sessions, and established an incident response plan.

- **Risk Communication:** Monthly risk reports helped management understand improvements and remaining challenges.

- **Outcome:** Over one year, the institution reduced successful phishing incidents by 40%.

Case Study 2: Global Healthcare Provider

A healthcare provider in Europe, aiming to comply with both HIPAA and GDPR, adopted a formal risk management framework:

- **Risk Identification:** Critical assets included patient records and diagnostic systems.

- **Risk Assessment:** They used a risk matrix to quantify risks and calculated ALE for key vulnerabilities.

- **Risk Mitigation:** Implemented encryption, upgraded legacy systems, and enforced strict access controls.

- **Risk Communication:** Developed dashboards to present risk levels to executive management.

- **Outcome:** The provider achieved a 50% reduction in security incidents and improved regulatory compliance, earning commendations during external audits.

3.6 Resources and Next Steps

To deepen your understanding of risk management in cyber defense, consider these resources:

- **Online Courses:**

  - Coursera, Udemy, and Cybrary offer courses on both qualitative and quantitative risk assessment techniques.

- **Books:**

  - *"Risk Management Framework: A Lab-Based Approach to Securing Information Systems"*

  - *"Managing Risk and Information Security: Protect to Enable"*

- **Certifications:**

- o Consider certifications like Certified Information Systems Risk Manager (CISRM) or CRISC.

- **Professional Organizations:**

  - o Engage with $(ISC)^2$, ISACA, or CompTIA for ongoing training and networking.

- **Websites and Blogs:**

  - o Visit NIST's Risk Management Framework pages and ISACA's risk management resources for the latest updates.

Practical Tip:

Begin by integrating simple risk management practices—such as periodic asset inventories and basic risk matrices—into your daily operations, then expand as you gain experience.

3.7 Chapter Takeaways

Key Points:

- **Risk management** transforms uncertainty into actionable intelligence through identification, assessment, mitigation, communication, and continuous monitoring.

- **Quantitative methods**, such as calculating Annualized Loss Expectancy (ALE), complement qualitative assessments and provide clear financial context.

- **Effective communication** of risk findings to stakeholders is crucial for obtaining support and driving action.

- **Integration of threat intelligence** enhances risk identification by keeping risk assessments current with emerging threats.

- Real-world case studies demonstrate how structured risk management improves security outcomes and compliance globally.

3.8 Test Your Knowledge

1. **What is the primary purpose of calculating Annualized Loss Expectancy (ALE) in risk management?**
   A. To eliminate risk entirely
   B. To quantify potential annual financial impact of risk
   C. To set up a risk matrix
   D. To transfer risk to a third party

2. **Which of the following best describes risk transfer?**
   A. Eliminating the risk by discontinuing a service
   B. Implementing controls to reduce the likelihood of an incident
   C. Shifting the risk to an external party through measures like insurance
   D. Accepting the risk as is because mitigation is costly

3. **Scenario Question:**
   Imagine you are responsible for risk management at a mid-sized retail company. You identify that a vulnerability in the payment system could lead to significant financial losses. How would you use threat intelligence to adjust your risk assessment, and which mitigation strategy (avoidance, reduction, transfer, or

acceptance) would you likely consider? Explain your reasoning briefly.

4. **Reflective Exercise:**
   List two assets from your professional or personal environment, identify one potential risk for each, and propose one risk mitigation strategy. Then, outline how you would communicate this risk to a non-technical stakeholder.

3.9 Final Thoughts

Risk management is not a one-time effort but an evolving process that must adapt to new threats and technologies. By systematically identifying, assessing, mitigating, and communicating risks, organizations can build a resilient defense against cyber-attacks. The techniques covered in this chapter—ranging from risk matrices and ALE calculations to integrating threat intelligence and effective risk communication—equip you with the tools to make informed decisions that enhance your overall security posture.

Reflect on the exercises provided and consider how you might implement these practices in your environment. As you move forward in this book, you'll see how these risk management principles tie into other aspects of cyber defense, such as incident response and threat intelligence. Your journey to mastering cyber defense continues with each proactive step you take toward understanding and managing risk.

Thank you for exploring Chapter 3. Use these insights to fortify digital defenses and prepare for the advanced topics ahead.

End of Chapter 3

Part 2: Core Pillars of Cyber Defense

Chapter 4: Network Security

Network security is a vital pillar of cyber defense, dedicated to protecting the digital highways that connect systems and users. It encompasses a range of technologies, policies, and best practices designed to safeguard data in transit, restrict unauthorized access, and detect malicious activity. In this chapter, we explore the core components and implementation strategies of network security. We build on the risk management insights from Chapter 3 and the foundational frameworks of Chapter 2, showing how to translate these principles into practical measures that secure both wired and wireless networks in today's dynamic threat landscape.

4.1 What Is Network Security?

Network security involves protecting digital communications and data transfers from unauthorized access, disruption, or exploitation. Think of it as the protective barrier around your organization's digital highways. Just as a physical security system uses locks, alarms, and surveillance to secure a building, network security deploys multiple defenses—ranging from firewalls to intrusion detection systems—to ensure that only legitimate traffic flows through your network.

By establishing layered defenses, network security ensures that even if one barrier is breached, additional measures help contain the threat. This approach is central to effective cyber defense, linking back to the defense-in-depth strategy introduced in Chapter 1 and the risk management frameworks discussed in Chapter 3.

Expert Insight:

"A secure network is the backbone of an effective cyber defense strategy. Without robust network security, even the best endpoint protections become ineffective." — Senior Network Security Architect

---

4.2 Core Components of Network Security

Modern network security relies on multiple, interlocking components. Each layer plays a specific role in safeguarding data and ensuring the overall integrity of your communications.

Firewalls

Firewalls are the first line of defense in controlling the flow of network traffic. There are several types:

- **Packet Filtering Firewalls:** These examine individual packets based on IP addresses, port numbers, and protocols.

- **Stateful Inspection Firewalls:** These track active connections and allow only packets that are part of a known session.

- **Next-Generation Firewalls (NGFW):** NGFWs go beyond traditional filtering by incorporating application-level inspection, intrusion prevention, and deep packet inspection to detect and block complex threats.

Intrusion Detection and Prevention Systems (IDS/IPS)

IDS and IPS monitor network traffic for suspicious behavior:

- **IDS:** Actively alert administrators when anomalies are detected.

- **IPS:** Take immediate action to block or mitigate threats in real time.

These systems are critical for early threat detection and response, providing the rapid reaction capabilities discussed in our risk management framework.

Virtual Private Networks (VPNs)

VPNs create encrypted tunnels for secure communication over public networks. They ensure that remote users and branch offices can connect safely, protecting sensitive data from interception and eavesdropping.

Network Segmentation and Micro-Segmentation

Segmenting a network limits the spread of attacks:

- **Traditional Segmentation:** Uses VLANs (Virtual Local Area Networks) to isolate different parts of the network.

- **Micro-Segmentation:** Provides granular control by dividing the network down to individual workloads, significantly reducing the attack surface.

A well-designed segmentation strategy prevents attackers from moving laterally within the network—a key risk reduction measure highlighted in Chapter 3.

Zero Trust Network Architecture

Zero Trust operates under the principle that no device or user is inherently trustworthy, regardless of their location. It requires continuous verification via strong authentication and authorization for every access request. This model minimizes lateral movement even if a breach occurs, reinforcing the layered defenses of network security.

Network Access Control (NAC)

NAC systems enforce security policies by ensuring that only compliant and authenticated devices gain network access. For example, before a device is allowed to connect, it might be required to run up-to-date antivirus software and have the latest security patches installed.

Wireless Network Security

With the growing importance of IoT and remote work, securing wireless networks has become critical:

- **Encryption Protocols:** Use WPA3 for robust wireless encryption.

- **Access Control:** Limit wireless access through strong authentication and MAC address filtering.

- **Monitoring:** Continuously monitor wireless traffic to detect rogue access points and unauthorized devices.

Secure Network Monitoring and SIEM Integration

Continuous monitoring is essential. SIEM (Security Information and Event Management) systems aggregate logs and events from multiple network devices (firewalls, routers, servers) to detect anomalies. For example, SIEM systems can help correlate unusual login attempts across different network segments. Effective SIEM integration involves gathering detailed logs— including authentication attempts, traffic anomalies, and configuration changes—to provide comprehensive visibility into network health.

4.3 Implementing Network Security in an Enterprise

Deploying a robust network security strategy involves careful planning, execution, and continuous improvement. Here's a structured approach:

Step 1: Network Inventory and Mapping

Start with a comprehensive inventory:

- **Hardware:** List routers, switches, servers, endpoints, IoT devices, and wireless access points.

- **Data Flows:** Create diagrams showing how information moves between systems.

- **Access Points:** Identify all entry and exit points, including VPN portals and wireless networks.

Example:
A network diagram might show the perimeter protected by an NGFW, internal segments divided by VLANs, and wireless access points connected to a separate guest network.

Step 2: Develop a Network Security Policy

Create clear policies outlining acceptable use, access controls, and security procedures. For instance, a policy review task could involve updating access controls to require multi-factor authentication for remote access.

Policy Example:
"All remote connections must use VPNs with multi-factor authentication and be monitored for suspicious activity."

Step 3: Deploy Security Technologies

Implement the core components discussed:

- **Firewalls:** Install and configure both traditional and next-generation firewalls at strategic points.

- **IDS/IPS:** Set up systems to detect and block threats.

- **VPNs:** Ensure all remote users connect via encrypted VPN tunnels.

- **Segmentation:** Apply network and micro-segmentation to contain potential breaches.

- **Wireless Security:** Secure wireless networks with WPA3 and restrict access.

- **Zero Trust & NAC:** Enforce strict identity verification and endpoint compliance.

- **SIEM Integration:** Collect and correlate logs for comprehensive monitoring.

Tip: Focus on gathering authentication logs, network traffic anomalies, and configuration change alerts.

Step 4: Continuous Monitoring and Updates

Use continuous monitoring tools to review network activity, adjust firewall rules, and perform periodic vulnerability assessments. Regular updates ensure that your security controls evolve with new threats.

Step 5: Employee Training and Awareness

Ensure that staff are trained in network security best practices. Regular sessions can cover topics like recognizing phishing attempts, securely configuring home networks for remote work, and following access control policies.

Actionable Task

- **Network Inventory Exercise:**
  Create a detailed list of all network devices and access points. Draw a network map that identifies critical assets, entry points, and data flow paths. For each segment, specify one security measure (e.g., "Deploy NGFW at the perimeter" or "Use WPA3 for wireless access").

- **Policy Review Task:**
  Review your current network security policy and identify one area for improvement. For instance, if remote access is not enforced with multi-factor authentication, draft a short plan outlining how to implement this control.

4.4 Real-World Applications and Case Studies

Case Study 1: Financial Institution Security Overhaul

A mid-sized financial institution recognized vulnerabilities in its traditional network design. To improve its defenses, the institution:

- **Segmented its Network:** Deployed VLANs to isolate sensitive financial data from general corporate traffic.

- **Upgraded Firewalls:** Installed NGFWs at strategic entry points to provide advanced threat detection.

- **Enhanced Monitoring:** Integrated a SIEM system to collect logs from multiple sources, enabling real-time anomaly detection.

- **Adopted Zero Trust:** Enforced continuous verification for remote access, requiring multi-factor authentication.

- **Wireless Security:** Secured its wireless networks by implementing WPA3 and monitoring for rogue access points.

Outcome: The institution reduced unauthorized access incidents by 45% and improved overall compliance with regulatory standards.

Case Study 2: Global E-Commerce Network Security

A large global e-commerce company faced challenges securing its diverse network that spanned data centers, cloud services, and remote users. Their strategy included:

- **Comprehensive Mapping:** Created detailed network diagrams outlining all segments and data flows.

- **Advanced VPN Solutions:** Deployed robust VPNs with strong encryption protocols for secure remote access.

- **Micro-Segmentation:** Divided the network into granular segments to limit lateral movement.

- **Wireless Network Enhancements:** Implemented stringent wireless security measures, including strong encryption and access control.

- **NAC Implementation:** Ensured only compliant devices could connect, verifying endpoints before network access.

- **Integrated Monitoring:** Used a SIEM system to gather logs on authentication, traffic anomalies, and configuration changes.

Outcome: The company achieved a 60% reduction in security incidents and bolstered its global compliance, particularly in regions with strict data protection laws such as under GDPR.

Global Insight:
A European e-commerce firm combined GDPR-driven policies with robust network segmentation, achieving a 50% reduction in data breach risks and setting an international benchmark for security excellence.

4.5 Resources and Next Steps

To continue building your network security expertise, explore the following resources:

- **Books:**

  - *"Network Security Essentials"*

  - *"Zero Trust Networks: Building Secure Systems in Untrusted Networks"*

- **Certifications:**

  - Consider obtaining certifications such as CISSP or Certified Ethical Hacker (CEH) for deeper technical proficiency.

- **Professional Organizations:**

  o Engage with (ISC)^2, ISACA, or CompTIA for networking, training, and up-to-date industry news.

- **Hands-On Tools:**

  o Explore open-source network simulators or SIEM tools (such as the ELK Stack) to gain practical experience.

Practical Tip:
Start by reviewing your existing network security measures and identify one immediate improvement—such as updating firewall rules or tightening wireless access controls—and set a timeline for implementation.

4.6 Chapter Takeaways

Key Points:

- **Network security** is essential for protecting digital communications and ensuring that data flows securely between devices and systems.

- Core components include **firewalls, IDS/IPS, VPNs, network segmentation, Zero Trust, NAC, wireless security,** and **SIEM integration**.

- A layered defense approach ensures that even if one security measure is breached, others help contain the threat.

- Implementation involves detailed network mapping, clear policies, deployment of security technologies, continuous monitoring, and employee training.

- Real-world case studies highlight measurable improvements such as a 45–60% reduction in security incidents and increased regulatory compliance.

4.7 Test Your Knowledge

1. **Which of the following best describes a Next-Generation Firewall (NGFW)?**
   A. A tool for basic packet filtering
   B. A system that performs deep packet inspection and advanced threat detection
   C. A simple VPN gateway
   D. A device solely used for network segmentation

2. **What is the primary purpose of network segmentation?**
   A. To simplify network administration
   B. To restrict lateral movement of attackers
   C. To enhance wireless signal strength
   D. To reduce the need for firewalls

3. **Scenario Question:**
   Imagine you are responsible for securing a multinational organization's network, which includes both wired and wireless components. Describe one strategy you would implement to prevent unauthorized access and explain how you would measure its effectiveness.

4. **Reflective Exercise:**
    Draw a basic network diagram of your current or an imagined environment. Identify key assets and entry points, then propose one security improvement for each segment. Finally, consider how you would update your network security policy to incorporate these changes.

4.8 Final Thoughts

Network security is not a one-off project but an ongoing process that must evolve with emerging threats and technologies. This chapter has provided a comprehensive look at the essential components, practical implementation steps, and real-world case studies that underscore the importance of securing digital communications. By integrating core technologies like firewalls, IDS/IPS, VPNs, and embracing advanced concepts such as Zero Trust and micro-segmentation, you can build a resilient network that not only protects your assets but also supports organizational growth and compliance.

Remember to revisit and update your network security measures regularly. As you continue with this book, the strategies discussed here will link to further topics such as incident response and threat intelligence, creating a cohesive and robust cyber defense framework.

Thank you for exploring Chapter 4. Your proactive steps today will help secure the digital highways of your organization and pave the way for a safer, more resilient future.

End of Chapter 4

Endpoint security is a critical pillar of cyber defense that focuses on protecting the devices used to access organizational networks and data. These devices—ranging from desktop computers and laptops to smartphones, tablets, and IoT gadgets—are often the primary entry points for cyber-attacks. In this chapter, we explore the core components of endpoint security, outline best practices and implementation strategies, and demonstrate how to secure endpoints effectively. Building on the foundational concepts and frameworks from earlier chapters, you'll learn practical steps to safeguard every device that connects to your network.

5.1 What Is Endpoint Security?

Endpoint security involves securing end-user devices against cyber threats, ensuring that each device accessing an organization's network is protected against malware, unauthorized access, and other forms of compromise. Consider endpoint security as the digital equivalent of personal security measures—just as you wouldn't leave your personal belongings unprotected, you must secure every device that connects to your organization.

Effective endpoint security combines a variety of technologies and policies to create a robust defense. It encompasses anti-virus software, endpoint detection and response (EDR) tools, device encryption, and strict access controls. By securing endpoints, organizations can prevent breaches that might otherwise lead to unauthorized network access, data loss, and other serious consequences.

Expert Insight:
"Endpoints are often the weakest link in an organization's security chain. Strengthening them is essential to building an overall resilient defense." — Senior Endpoint Security Specialist

---

5.2 Core Components of Endpoint Security

Modern endpoint security is built upon multiple layers, each designed to protect devices from different angles. Here are the key components:

Anti-Virus and Anti-Malware Software

- **Purpose:** Detect and remove malicious software.

- **Functionality:** Scans files, monitors system behavior, and provides real-time protection against viruses, spyware, ransomware, and other malware.

Endpoint Detection and Response (EDR)

- **Purpose:** Offer advanced monitoring and threat detection capabilities.

- **Functionality:** Continuously monitors endpoints for suspicious activity, provides detailed forensic data, and supports rapid incident response.

- **Advantage:** EDR solutions go beyond traditional anti-virus by detecting sophisticated, stealthy threats.

Device Encryption

- **Purpose:** Protect data at rest on endpoint devices.

- **Functionality:** Uses encryption algorithms (e.g., AES) to ensure that sensitive data is inaccessible without proper decryption keys.

- **Example:** Full disk encryption on laptops ensures that even if a device is stolen, the data remains secure.

Application Control and Allow-listing

- **Purpose:** Restrict which applications can run on a device.

- **Functionality:** Only approved, trusted applications are allowed to execute, minimizing the risk of malware installation.

- **Tip:** Application allow-listing is especially effective in environments with strict operational requirements.

Patch Management

- **Purpose:** Keep endpoint software up to date.

- **Functionality:** Regularly updates operating systems and applications to fix vulnerabilities that attackers could exploit.

- **Challenge:** Timely patch deployment is crucial, as delays can leave endpoints exposed to known threats.

Mobile Device Management (MDM)

- **Purpose:** Secure and manage mobile endpoints.

- **Functionality:** Enforces security policies, manages device settings, and allows remote monitoring and control of mobile devices.

- **Importance:** With the rise of remote work and BYOD (Bring Your Own Device) policies, MDM has become essential.

Data Loss Prevention (DLP) on Endpoints

- **Purpose:** Prevent unauthorized data transfer.

- **Functionality:** Monitors and controls data movement on endpoints, ensuring that sensitive information does not leave the device without proper authorization.

- **Benefit:** DLP helps mitigate insider threats and accidental data exposure.

5.3 Implementing Endpoint Security

Deploying an effective endpoint security strategy requires a systematic approach that integrates technology, policy, and continuous monitoring. Here's a step-by-step guide to implementation:

Step 1: Inventory and Classification

Begin by identifying and classifying all endpoints within your organization:

- **Asset Inventory:** Document all devices, including desktops, laptops, mobile devices, and IoT gadgets.

- **Classification:** Group endpoints by risk level and criticality (e.g., devices handling sensitive data versus general office devices).

Step 2: Develop an Endpoint Security Policy

Establish clear policies that define:

- **Device Usage:** Acceptable use guidelines and security requirements for all endpoints.

- **Access Controls:** Requirements for multi-factor authentication and role-based access.

- **Compliance Standards:** Alignment with broader frameworks (e.g., NIST, ISO/IEC 27001) and regulatory mandates.

Step 3: Deploy and Configure Security Solutions

Implement the core components discussed:

- **Anti-Virus/EDR:** Install and configure solutions to provide real-time protection and advanced threat detection.

- **Encryption:** Enforce full disk encryption on all portable devices.

- **Application Allow-listing:** Configure allow-listing to restrict unauthorized software.

- **MDM Solutions:** Deploy MDM tools to manage mobile devices and enforce security policies.

- **Patch Management Systems:** Automate updates to ensure timely patch deployment.

Step 4: Monitor, Analyze, and Respond

Integrate endpoint security tools with centralized monitoring systems:

- **SIEM Integration:** Collect logs from endpoint security tools to correlate events and detect anomalies.

- **Continuous Monitoring:** Use EDR and MDM systems to track device health and security status.

- **Incident Response:** Develop and test an endpoint-specific response plan for rapid containment and remediation of breaches.

Step 5: Regular Training and Policy Review

Educate users on endpoint security best practices and update policies regularly:

- **User Training:** Regular sessions on recognizing phishing attempts, safe browsing, and secure device usage.

- **Policy Audits:** Periodically review and update security policies based on emerging threats and technological advances.

Actionable Task

- **Endpoint Inventory Exercise:**
  Create a list of all endpoints in your organization. For each device, note its criticality, current security measures (anti-virus, encryption status), and any potential vulnerabilities (e.g., outdated software).

- **Mitigation Planning:**
  Select one high-risk endpoint from your list and draft a detailed plan to address its vulnerabilities. Consider measures such as enhanced patch management, additional encryption, or stricter access controls.

Include a timeline and assign responsibilities for implementation.

5.4 Real-World Applications and Case Studies

Case Study 1: Strengthening Endpoint Security at a Financial Institution

A mid-sized financial institution, after several security incidents, revamped its endpoint security:

- **Deployment of EDR:** The institution installed an advanced EDR solution across all endpoints, enabling real-time threat detection and automated response.

- **Encryption Enforcement:** Full disk encryption was mandated for all laptops and mobile devices.

- **User Training:** Regular training sessions reduced the incidence of malware infections and phishing-related breaches.

- **Outcome:** The institution reported a 50% reduction in endpoint-related security incidents and improved regulatory compliance, contributing to enhanced customer trust.

Case Study 2: Securing a Global Retail Chain's Mobile Devices

A global retail chain with a vast number of mobile devices implemented a comprehensive MDM solution:

- **MDM Deployment:** All employee smartphones and tablets were enrolled in the MDM system, ensuring consistent security configurations.

- **Application Control:** The chain enforced application allow-listing, preventing unauthorized apps from being installed.

- **Patch Management:** Automated patch updates minimized the risk of vulnerabilities.

- **Outcome:** The retail chain achieved a 60% reduction in mobile security incidents, with enhanced protection of customer data and smoother regulatory audits.

Global Insight:
A European retailer integrated GDPR compliance with robust endpoint security measures, including encryption and MDM, reducing endpoint breaches by 55% and setting a benchmark in cross-border data protection.

5.5 Resources and Next Steps

To further your expertise in endpoint security, consider these resources:

- **Online Courses:**

  - Platforms like Coursera, Udemy, and Cybrary offer courses specifically on endpoint security, EDR, and mobile device management.

- **Books:**

  - *"Endpoint Security: A Comprehensive Guide"*

  - *"Mastering Endpoint Detection and Response"*

- **Certifications:**

- Explore certifications such as Certified Endpoint Security Professional (CESP) or Certified Ethical Hacker (CEH) for a deeper dive.

- **Professional Organizations:**

  - Engage with $(ISC)^2$, ISACA, or CompTIA for continuing education and industry insights.

- **Hands-On Tools:**

  - Experiment with open-source endpoint security tools and network simulators to gain practical experience.

Practical Tip:
Begin by conducting a thorough inventory of all endpoints in your organization. Identify one immediate improvement—such as enforcing encryption on portable devices—and plan its implementation with a clear timeline.

5.6 Chapter Takeaways

Key Points:

- **Endpoint security** is critical for protecting all devices that connect to your organization, from desktops and laptops to mobile devices and IoT gadgets.

- Core components include **anti-virus/EDR, encryption, application allow-listing, MDM, patch management**, and **DLP** for endpoints.

- Effective endpoint security requires a layered approach that combines technology, policies, continuous monitoring, and user education.

- Real-world case studies illustrate significant reductions in security incidents and enhanced compliance through robust endpoint security measures.

- Integrating endpoint security with centralized monitoring (SIEM) and regular policy reviews ensures adaptive and responsive protection.

5.7 Test Your Knowledge

1. **Which of the following is a primary function of an Endpoint Detection and Response (EDR) solution?**
   A. Encrypting data at rest
   B. Monitoring endpoints for suspicious activity and providing forensic data
   C. Restricting software installations through allow-listing
   D. Managing mobile device policies

2. **What is the main goal of using Mobile Device Management (MDM) in endpoint security?**
   A. To speed up network connectivity
   B. To enforce security policies and monitor mobile endpoints
   C. To replace traditional anti-virus software
   D. To enable file sharing among employees

3. **Scenario Question:**
   Imagine you are responsible for securing endpoints in a multinational company. Describe one strategy you would implement to ensure that devices remain updated and protected against known vulnerabilities and explain how you would measure its effectiveness.

4. **Reflective Exercise:**
   List two types of endpoints in your organization, identify a key risk associated with each, and propose one mitigation strategy. Then, outline how you would communicate these risks and mitigations to non-technical stakeholders.

5.8 Final Thoughts

Endpoint security is a vital element in creating a resilient cyber defense strategy. By securing every device that accesses your network, you prevent attackers from exploiting weak links to compromise your entire infrastructure. This chapter has provided an in-depth look at the technologies, best practices, and strategies essential for effective endpoint security—from anti-virus and EDR solutions to encryption, MDM, and patch management.

Remember, endpoint security is an ongoing process that requires continuous monitoring, regular updates, and proactive user training. As you move forward in this book, the concepts and strategies discussed here will interconnect with other core areas like network security, risk management, and incident response to create a comprehensive defense framework.

Thank you for exploring Chapter 5. Take these insights and actionable tasks into your daily operations and strengthen the security of every device in your organization. Your proactive approach to endpoint security is a key step toward building a robust, resilient cyber defense.

End of Chapter 5

Identity and Access Management (IAM) is a cornerstone of modern cyber defense, ensuring that only authorized individuals gain access to sensitive systems and data. In this chapter, we build on the foundational concepts from Chapters 1–5—linking risk management and endpoint security to IAM—to provide a comprehensive guide on managing digital identities. You will learn core IAM components, discover actionable implementation strategies, and explore real-world case studies that illustrate how effective IAM practices can dramatically reduce risks. We also examine emerging trends such as passwordless and decentralized identity, preparing you for the future of access management.

6.1 What Is Identity and Access Management (IAM)?

IAM is the framework of policies, technologies, and processes used to manage digital identities and control user access to resources. It ensures that the right individuals access the right resources at the right time and for the right reasons. In practice, IAM involves:

- **Authentication:** Verifying user identities through passwords, tokens, or biometrics.

- **Authorization:** Granting appropriate access levels based on defined roles.

- **Identity Governance:** Overseeing the creation, modification, and deletion of digital identities.

- **Auditing:** Monitoring access and usage to detect anomalies and ensure compliance.

IAM is crucial because it reduces the attack surface by enforcing the principle of least privilege and preventing unauthorized access. Whether securing employee accounts or customer data, a robust IAM strategy is essential to protect against both external and insider threats.

Expert Insight:
"IAM is not just about managing passwords; it's about managing every digital identity across your enterprise, ensuring that access is continuously verified and dynamically adjusted based on risk." — Chief Information Security Officer

---

6.2 Core Components of IAM

Modern IAM systems integrate multiple layers to provide comprehensive protection. The key components include:

Multi-Factor Authentication (MFA)

- **Purpose:** Strengthen authentication by requiring two or more verification methods.

- **Example:** Combining a password (something you know) with a smartphone token (something you have) or biometric data (something you are).

- **Emerging Trend:** Passwordless authentication is gaining traction, where biometrics or hardware tokens replace traditional passwords.

Single Sign-On (SSO)

- **Purpose:** Allow users to access multiple applications with a single set of credentials.

- **Benefit:** Reduces password fatigue and limits the risk of password reuse.

- **Example:** A user logs into an enterprise portal (e.g., via Microsoft Azure AD or Okta) and gains seamless access to email, CRM, and collaboration tools.

Role-Based Access Control (RBAC)

- **Purpose:** Assign permissions based on user roles, ensuring users only access what they need.

- **Example:** A finance team member is granted access to financial systems but not to HR or IT systems.

- **Policy Tip:** A "least privilege" policy ensures that roles are defined with the minimum access necessary.

Privileged Access Management (PAM)

- **Purpose:** Secure and monitor accounts with elevated privileges.

- **Function:** PAM tools control and audit access to sensitive administrative accounts, reducing the risk of insider abuse.

- **Example:** Tools like CyberArk or BeyondTrust help enforce and monitor privileged access.

Identity Governance and Administration (IGA)

- **Purpose:** Oversee the lifecycle of digital identities—from creation to de-provisioning.

- **Key Functions:** Automate account provisioning, enforce policy compliance, and perform regular access reviews.

- **Integration:** IGA solutions often connect with directory services like Active Directory, streamlining user provisioning and deprovisioning.

Biometric Authentication

- **Purpose:** Utilize unique biological characteristics (fingerprints, facial recognition) to verify identity.

- **Advantage:** Offers a higher assurance level compared to traditional passwords.

- **Trend:** Increasing adoption in mobile and high-security environments.

Directory Services Integration

- **Purpose:** Centralize identity data using systems like Active Directory or LDAP.

- **Benefit:** Provides a single source of truth, simplifying user management and policy enforcement.

- **Example:** Integration with Active Directory can automate user provisioning, deprovisioning, and access reviews.

6.3 Implementing IAM in an Enterprise

Deploying a robust IAM strategy requires a systematic, multi-phase approach that aligns with broader risk management and endpoint security strategies.

Step 1: Inventory and Classification

- **Digital Identity Inventory:**
  Compile a comprehensive list of all users, including employees, contractors, partners, and customers.

- **Device and Application Mapping:**
  Identify which devices and applications each identity accesses.

- **Risk Classification:**
  Group identities by criticality and access level—distinguishing high-risk administrative accounts from general user accounts.

Step 2: Policy Development and Governance

- **Access Control Policies:**
  Define clear rules for access. For example, establish a policy stating that "All users must have multi-factor authentication enabled, and access must be granted based on the principle of least privilege."

- **Authentication Policies:**
  Specify requirements for MFA, SSO, and even emerging passwordless methods.

- **Regular Reviews:**
  Set a schedule to review and update policies to reflect changes in technology, threat landscape, and regulatory requirements.

Step 3: Deploy IAM Technologies

- **Implement MFA and SSO:**
  Deploy solutions (e.g., Okta, Azure AD) that provide robust MFA and SSO capabilities to simplify access while enhancing security.

- **Configure RBAC and PAM:**
  Establish roles and permissions based on job functions. Integrate PAM solutions to monitor and restrict access for privileged accounts.

- **Integrate IGA with Directory Services:**
  Use IGA tools to automate the provisioning and deprovisioning of accounts. Integrate with Active Directory for centralized management.

- **Adopt Biometric and Passwordless Solutions:**
  Where possible, incorporate biometric authentication to further strengthen identity verification.

Step 4: Continuous Monitoring and Auditing

- **Audit Trails:**
  Implement logging to track user access and behavior. Regular audits help identify policy violations or anomalies.

- **Real-Time Alerts:**
  Set up automated alerts for unusual access patterns, such as multiple failed login attempts or logins from unexpected locations.

- **Periodic Assessments:**
  Regularly assess IAM configurations through internal audits and penetration tests.

Step 5: Training and Awareness

- **User Training:**
  Conduct regular training on IAM best practices, including safe password management and recognizing phishing attempts.

- **Administrator Training:**
  Provide specialized training for those managing IAM systems, emphasizing emerging trends like decentralized identity.

Actionable Task

- **IAM Inventory Exercise:**
  Develop an inventory of all digital identities in your organization. Classify each identity by risk level and list the applications and devices they access. Select one high-risk identity and draft a plan to enhance its security—consider enforcing MFA and reviewing its access privileges.

- **Policy Drafting Exercise:**
  Choose one key policy area (e.g., RBAC) and create an outline that defines user roles, minimum necessary permissions, and the process for periodic review. Write a sample policy statement that can be communicated to both technical and non-technical stakeholders.

6.4 Real-World Applications and Case Studies

Case Study 1: Financial Institution Enhances IAM

A mid-sized bank implemented a comprehensive IAM solution to secure sensitive financial data:

- **MFA Deployment:**
  The bank adopted Okta for MFA, requiring all
  employees to use a combination of passwords and
  mobile authentication.

- **RBAC Implementation:**
  Roles were redefined to ensure that only users in
  finance had access to critical financial systems, while
  other departments were restricted.

- **PAM Integration:**
  Privileged accounts were managed using CyberArk,
  ensuring that administrative access was closely
  monitored.

- **Outcome:**
  The bank experienced a 40% reduction in unauthorized
  access incidents and improved compliance with
  financial regulations, boosting stakeholder confidence.

Case Study 2: Healthcare Provider Adopts Advanced IAM

A European healthcare provider revamped its IAM strategy to
meet stringent GDPR and HIPAA requirements:

- **IGA Automation:**
  The provider integrated Microsoft Azure AD with its
  IGA solution, automating user provisioning and
  deprovisioning processes.

- **SSO Implementation:**
  SSO was deployed to streamline access for healthcare
  professionals while ensuring robust security.

- **Biometric Authentication:**
  High-security areas were secured using biometric methods, enhancing the protection of patient records.

- **Outcome:**
  The organization achieved a 50% reduction in access-related incidents and significantly improved regulatory compliance, leading to better patient trust.

Global Insight:
An international retail corporation integrated advanced IAM practices, including passwordless authentication and decentralized identity models, across its global operations. This approach not only reduced access-related incidents by 55% but also set a benchmark for innovative identity management in a competitive market.

6.5 Resources and Next Steps

To deepen your IAM expertise, consider the following resources:

- **Books:**

  - *"Identity and Access Management: Business Performance Through Connected Intelligence"*

  - *"Modern Identity: How to Manage and Secure Your Digital Identities"*

- **Certifications:**

  - Explore certifications such as Certified Identity and Access Manager (CIAM) or those offered by (ISC)^2.

- **Professional Organizations:**

    o Engage with ISACA, (ISC)^2, or CompTIA for continuous training, networking, and updates.

- **Tools for Hands-On Practice:**

    o Experiment with open-source IAM tools like Keycloak or trial versions of commercial solutions to gain practical experience.

Practical Tip:
Begin with a pilot project—select a department or a specific group of users to implement MFA and SSO. Monitor the results and use the insights to scale the IAM solution organization wide.

6.6 Chapter Takeaways

Key Points:

- **IAM** is critical for controlling access to digital resources by managing identities and enforcing appropriate access policies.

- Core components include **MFA, SSO, RBAC, PAM, IGA, biometric authentication,** and **directory services integration**.

- Effective implementation of IAM requires a systematic approach: inventory and classification, policy development, technology deployment, continuous monitoring, and regular training.

- Real-world case studies demonstrate significant improvements—such as 40–50% reductions in unauthorized access—when robust IAM strategies are applied.

- Emerging trends like passwordless authentication and decentralized identity are shaping the future of IAM.

6.7 Test Your Knowledge

1. **Which of the following best describes a primary function of Multi-Factor Authentication (MFA)?**
   A. Simplifying access across applications
   B. Strengthening authentication by requiring multiple verification methods
   C. Managing user roles and permissions
   D. Encrypting data on devices

2. **What is the main goal of Role-Based Access Control (RBAC) in an IAM system?**
   A. To provide a single sign-on experience
   B. To assign permissions based on user roles, enforcing the principle of least privilege
   C. To monitor network traffic
   D. To store user passwords securely

3. **Scenario Question:**
   Imagine you are the IT manager at a multinational organization. You need to secure access for both on-premise and cloud-based systems. Describe one strategy (e.g., implementing SSO or PAM) you would deploy, and explain how it would address both usability and security. Provide specific details, such as the potential use of tools like Okta or Azure AD.

4. **Reflective Exercise:**
   List two common risks associated with poor IAM practices (e.g., excessive privileges or unmonitored access). For each risk, propose a mitigation strategy and outline how you would communicate these risks and strategies to non-technical stakeholders.

6.8 Final Thoughts

Identity and Access Management is at the heart of an effective cyber defense strategy. By ensuring that only authorized individuals can access sensitive systems and data, IAM minimizes risks and strengthens organizational security. This chapter has provided a detailed exploration of IAM concepts, from core components and implementation strategies to real-world case studies and emerging trends like passwordless authentication.

As you move forward in this book, the principles of IAM will interconnect with other aspects of cyber defense, such as endpoint security and risk management, creating a holistic and robust defense framework. Your proactive steps in adopting strong IAM practices—combined with continuous monitoring and regular policy updates—will not only enhance security but also build trust and compliance across your organization.

Thank you for exploring Chapter 6. Apply these insights and actionable tasks to elevate your IAM strategy and continue your journey toward mastering cyber defense.

End of Chapter 6

Data protection is a fundamental element of cyber defense, focused on safeguarding the confidentiality, integrity, and availability of information. As organizations generate and process ever-increasing amounts of data, protecting that data against loss, corruption, and unauthorized access becomes critical. In this chapter, we explore the key concepts, technologies, and strategies used to protect data—both in storage and during transmission. Building on the previous chapters that covered frameworks, risk management, network security, endpoint security, and IAM, we now dive into practical measures for ensuring data remains secure. We also examine real-world case studies and provide actionable tasks to help you implement robust data protection practices.

7.1 What Is Data Protection?

Data protection encompasses the policies, procedures, and technologies that are put in place to secure data throughout its lifecycle—from creation and storage to transmission and deletion. Its primary goals are to ensure:

- **Confidentiality:** Sensitive data is accessible only to authorized users.

- **Integrity:** Data remains accurate, consistent, and unaltered.

- **Availability:** Data is accessible when needed, even in the event of a disruption.

Effective data protection is not limited to digital encryption; it includes strategies such as Data Loss Prevention (DLP), secure backups, and data classification. In today's threat landscape, protecting data means defending against cyber-attacks, accidental loss, and even insider threats.

Expert Insight:
"Data is the lifeblood of modern organizations. Without effective data protection, even the most sophisticated cyber defenses are rendered useless." — Chief Information Security Officer

---

7.2 Core Components of Data Protection

Modern data protection is built on a multi-layered approach that involves both technical solutions and policy-driven controls. The key components include:

Encryption

- **Purpose:** Encrypt data at rest and in transit to render it unreadable without the proper decryption keys.

- **Techniques:**

  - **Symmetric Encryption:** Algorithms like AES are favored for their efficiency and security.

  - **Asymmetric Encryption:** RSA and ECC are used for secure key exchanges and digital signatures.

  - **Advanced Concepts:** Homomorphic encryption, which allows computations on encrypted data, is emerging as a promising technique for maintaining privacy in cloud environments.

- **Use Case:** Encrypting sensitive files stored on servers and ensuring that data transmitted over networks is secure from eavesdropping.

Data Loss Prevention (DLP)

- **Purpose:** Prevent unauthorized data exfiltration and ensure that sensitive information does not leave the organization.

- **Capabilities:**

  - Monitoring and controlling data transfers across endpoints, networks, and cloud environments.

  - Enforcing policies that restrict data sharing based on content analysis.

- **Tools:** Solutions like Symantec DLP or Digital Guardian help organizations enforce these policies.

- **Example:** Preventing an employee from emailing unencrypted sensitive customer data outside the organization.

Data Classification and Tokenization

- **Data Classification:**

  - **Purpose:** Categorize data based on sensitivity and regulatory requirements.

  - **Process:** Identify and label data (e.g., public, internal, confidential, or restricted) to apply appropriate protection measures.

- **Tokenization:**

- Purpose: Replace sensitive data with non-sensitive tokens that can be mapped back to the original data under controlled conditions.

- Advantage: Reduces the exposure of sensitive information during processing and storage.

Backup and Disaster Recovery

- **Purpose:** Ensure that data is not permanently lost and can be restored following an incident.

- **Approaches:**

    - **Regular Backups:** Scheduled backups of critical data to secure, offsite locations.

    - **Redundancy:** Use of multiple storage systems and cloud services to ensure availability.

    - **Disaster Recovery Plans:** Detailed strategies to restore data and operations quickly after a breach, system failure, or natural disaster.

- **Example:** Implementing automated backup solutions that create encrypted copies of data every 24 hours.

Data Governance and Compliance

- **Purpose:** Ensure that data protection practices align with regulatory requirements (e.g., GDPR, HIPAA, PCI-DSS) and internal policies.

- **Key Functions:**

    - Establish data handling and retention policies.

- o Conduct regular audits and assessments to verify compliance.

- o Educate employees on data protection best practices.

- **Outcome:** Improved accountability and reduced risk of non-compliance fines.

7.3 Implementing Data Protection

A robust data protection strategy is not built overnight—it requires a structured approach that integrates technology, policies, and continuous monitoring. Here's a step-by-step guide to implementing effective data protection measures:

Step 1: Data Inventory and Classification

- **Asset Inventory:**
  Compile a detailed inventory of all data assets, including databases, files, and cloud-stored information.

- **Classification:**
  Categorize data based on sensitivity (e.g., public, internal, confidential, restricted) to determine the level of protection required.

- **Task:**
  Create a data inventory spreadsheet that includes data type, storage location, owner, and classification level.

Step 2: Policy Development

- **Data Handling Policies:**
  Define how data should be stored, accessed, transmitted, and disposed of securely.

- **Encryption Policies:**
  Establish rules for when and how data must be encrypted (e.g., all sensitive data must be encrypted both at rest and in transit).

- **DLP Policies:**
  Develop guidelines to monitor and control the movement of sensitive data.

- **Example Policy Statement:**
  "All confidential data must be encrypted using AES-256 before being stored or transmitted. Unauthorized sharing of such data is strictly prohibited."

Step 3: Deploying Technical Controls

- **Encryption Tools:**
  Implement encryption solutions for both data at rest and in transit. This may involve using disk encryption tools for endpoints and secure protocols (like TLS) for network communications.

- **DLP Solutions:**
  Install DLP software to monitor data movement across endpoints, networks, and cloud services. Configure the system to block or alert on unauthorized data transfers.

- **Backup Systems:**
  Set up automated backup solutions that encrypt data

and store it in multiple secure locations. Test your disaster recovery plan regularly.

- **Tokenization and Classification Tools:**
  Use software to automate data classification and tokenization, reducing manual errors and ensuring consistency.

- **Integration:**
  Integrate these solutions with existing IT systems and ensure they work cohesively with risk management, network security, and IAM frameworks.

Step 4: Continuous Monitoring and Auditing

- **Real-Time Monitoring:**
  Use SIEM systems to collect logs and monitor data flows for unusual activity. This helps in early detection of data breaches.

- **Regular Audits:**
  Schedule periodic audits of data protection controls to ensure policies are followed and tools are updated.

- **Automated Alerts:**
  Configure alerts for potential data leaks or unauthorized access and establish protocols for rapid response.

Step 5: Training and Awareness

- **Employee Training:**
  Educate staff on data protection best practices, including how to handle sensitive data and respond to security incidents.

- **Awareness Programs:**
  Regularly update employees on new threats and the importance of following data protection policies.

- **Role-Specific Training:**
  Provide specialized training for roles that handle sensitive data or manage backup systems.

Actionable Task

- **Data Protection Inventory Exercise:**
  Develop an inventory of your organization's data assets, classifying each according to sensitivity. For one high-risk data category, draft a plan that outlines encryption methods, backup frequency, and DLP controls.

- **Policy Drafting Exercise:**
  Choose one key area—such as data encryption—and write a sample policy statement that includes specific technical requirements (e.g., "All credit card data must be encrypted with AES-256 and tokenized before processing."). Share this draft with both technical and non-technical stakeholders for feedback.

7.4 Real-World Applications and Case Studies

Case Study 1: Enhancing Data Protection in a Financial Institution

A mid-sized bank, facing increasing regulatory scrutiny, revamped its data protection strategy:

- **Encryption Implementation:**
  The bank deployed enterprise-grade encryption for all

data at rest using AES-256 and secured data in transit via TLS.

- **DLP Deployment:**
  A robust DLP solution was installed to monitor data transfers and prevent unauthorized sharing of sensitive customer information.

- **Backup and Recovery:**
  Automated, encrypted backups were scheduled daily, with offsite storage to ensure data availability during disasters.

- **Outcome:**
  The bank reported a 50% reduction in data breach incidents, improved compliance with financial regulations, and enhanced customer trust.

Case Study 2: Secure Data Management in a Global Retail Chain

A global e-commerce company needed to protect vast amounts of customer data while complying with international privacy regulations like GDPR:

- **Data Classification and Tokenization:**
  The company implemented a data classification system that automatically labeled data based on sensitivity, and tokenized sensitive customer information.

- **Integrated Data Governance:**
  Comprehensive policies were developed and enforced to ensure proper data handling, retention, and secure disposal.

- **Outcome:**
  The company achieved a 60% reduction in data leak incidents and streamlined its compliance processes across multiple jurisdictions.

Global Insight:
A European technology firm combined advanced encryption techniques with rigorous data governance policies, reducing data exposure risks by 55% and setting a new industry standard for compliance and resilience.

7.5 Resources and Next Steps

To deepen your knowledge and improve your data protection strategies, explore these resources:

- **Online Courses:**
  - Platforms like Coursera, Udemy, and Cybrary offer courses on data protection fundamentals, encryption technologies, and DLP strategies.

- **Books:**
  - *"Data Protection: A Practical Guide"*
  - *"Encryption and Data Security for the Enterprise"*

- **Certifications:**
  - Consider certifications such as Certified Data Privacy Solutions Engineer (CDPSE) or Certified Information Privacy Professional (CIPP).

- **Professional Organizations:**

- Engage with ISACA, (ISC)^2, and the IAPP for training, networking, and updates on data protection best practices.

- **Tools:**

  - Experiment with open-source encryption tools, DLP solutions, or backup software to gain hands-on experience.

Practical Tip:
Start by performing a data inventory and classification exercise. Identify one critical data asset and implement encryption and DLP controls for it, then measure the impact over a set period.

7.6 Chapter Takeaways

Key Points:

- **Data protection** safeguards the confidentiality, integrity, and availability of information through encryption, DLP, and robust backup strategies.

- Core components include **encryption, data classification, tokenization, DLP, backup and disaster recovery,** and **data governance.**

- Effective implementation requires a systematic approach: inventory and classification, policy development, deployment of technical controls, continuous monitoring, and user training.

- Real-world case studies show that structured data protection strategies can lead to significant reductions in data breach incidents and enhanced regulatory compliance.

- Emerging trends like passwordless and decentralized identity are shaping the future of data protection.

7.7 Test Your Knowledge

1. **What is the primary purpose of encrypting data at rest and in transit?**
A. To prevent unauthorized access by making data unreadable without a decryption key
B. To increase data storage capacity
C. To improve network speed
D. To comply with data classification standards

2. **Which of the following best describes Data Loss Prevention (DLP)?**
A. A tool for encrypting sensitive data
B. A system for monitoring and controlling data transfers
C. A method for classifying data
D. A backup solution for disaster recovery

3. **Scenario Question:**
Imagine you are the IT manager for a multinational corporation. You identify that unencrypted customer data poses a significant risk during transmission. Describe one strategy you would implement to address this risk and explain how you would measure its effectiveness. Include potential tools or encryption protocols that might be used.

4. **Reflective Exercise:**
   List two types of data (e.g., customer financial records and employee HR files) within your organization. For each, identify a potential risk and propose one mitigation strategy. Finally, outline how you would communicate these risks and your mitigation plan to non-technical stakeholders.

7.8 Final Thoughts

Data protection is an essential pillar of cyber defense that ensures your most valuable asset—information—is secured against a multitude of threats. This chapter has provided a comprehensive overview of the strategies and technologies used to protect data, from robust encryption and DLP solutions to effective backup and recovery practices. The systematic approach detailed here—from data inventory and classification to policy development, technical control deployment, continuous monitoring, and user training—empowers you to build a resilient data protection strategy.

As you progress in this book, the data protection concepts discussed here will integrate with other core areas, such as risk management, network security, and endpoint security, forming a holistic and robust defense framework. By staying proactive and embracing emerging trends, you can ensure that your organization's data remains secure, compliant, and resilient against evolving cyber threats.

Thank you for exploring Chapter 7. Apply these insights and actionable tasks to enhance your data protection practices and continue your journey toward mastering cyber defense.

End of Chapter 7

Application security is a critical element of cyber defense that focuses on safeguarding software applications from vulnerabilities, exploits, and attacks. In today's digital landscape, applications are prime targets for cybercriminals, making it essential to integrate security practices throughout the software development lifecycle (SDLC). This chapter delves into the core components of application security, outlines best practices and implementation strategies, and illustrates these concepts through real-world case studies. Building on the foundations laid in previous chapters, you will learn how to secure your applications from design to deployment and beyond.

8.1 What Is Application Security?

Application security refers to the measures and processes implemented to prevent, detect, and remediate vulnerabilities within software applications. It spans the entire SDLC—from design and development to testing, deployment, and maintenance. The primary goals are to ensure that applications remain secure against threats and that any potential vulnerabilities are identified and mitigated before they can be exploited by attackers.

Key objectives of application security include:

- **Confidentiality:** Preventing unauthorized access to sensitive data processed or stored by applications.

- **Integrity:** Ensuring that the application's data and functionality are not altered in an unauthorized manner.

- **Availability:** Guaranteeing that the application remains functional and accessible, even under attack.

Effective application security is achieved by embedding security practices into every phase of the SDLC, thereby creating a "shift-left" approach that reduces the window of vulnerability.

Expert Insight:
"Application security is not an afterthought; it must be an integral part of the development process. Secure coding, regular testing, and continuous monitoring are the keys to building resilient applications." — Lead Security Engineer

---

8.2 Core Components of Application Security

A robust application security strategy consists of multiple layers that work together to mitigate risks. The key components include:

Secure Coding Practices

- **Principles:**
  Adopt secure coding standards (e.g., OWASP Secure Coding Practices) to minimize vulnerabilities from the outset.

- **Practices:**

  - Validate all inputs to prevent injection attacks.

  - Employ error handling that does not disclose sensitive information.

  - Avoid hard-coding sensitive data (e.g., credentials) in source code.

Static Application Security Testing (SAST)

- **Purpose:**
  Analyze source code or binaries for vulnerabilities without executing the application.

- **Tools:**
  Use tools such as SonarQube or Checkmarx to identify coding errors and security weaknesses early in the development cycle.

- **Benefit:**
  Detect vulnerabilities before the application is deployed, reducing remediation costs.

Dynamic Application Security Testing (DAST)

- **Purpose:**
  Test running applications to identify vulnerabilities that manifest during execution.

- **Tools:**
  Tools like OWASP ZAP or Burp Suite simulate attacks on live applications.

- **Advantage:**
  Helps in uncovering issues that static analysis might miss, such as runtime errors and configuration issues.

Penetration Testing

- **Purpose:**
  Simulate real-world attacks to assess the security posture of applications.

- **Process:**
  Engage ethical hackers to identify and exploit

vulnerabilities, then document findings and recommend remediation.

- **Outcome:**
Provides a comprehensive view of potential attack vectors and demonstrates the effectiveness of existing security measures.

Web Application Firewalls (WAF)

- **Purpose:**
Monitor and filter HTTP traffic between web applications and the Internet.

- **Functionality:**
Block common web exploits and provide an additional layer of defense against attacks such as SQL injection and cross-site scripting (XSS).

- **Deployment:**
WAFs can be deployed as hardware appliances, cloud services, or integrated within the application architecture.

DevSecOps and Continuous Security Testing

- **Integration:**
Embed security into DevOps practices by automating security tests throughout the SDLC.

- **Benefits:**
Continuous integration and continuous deployment (CI/CD) pipelines incorporate automated SAST and DAST tools, ensuring that security is maintained without slowing development.

- **Emerging Trend:**
  Shift-left security practices focus on early detection and remediation of vulnerabilities.

Runtime Application Self-Protection (RASP)

- **Purpose:**
  Monitor and protect applications in real-time during runtime.

- **Functionality:**
  RASP solutions integrate with the application runtime to detect and mitigate threats as they occur, offering adaptive protection against zero-day vulnerabilities.

8.3 Implementing Application Security

Implementing an effective application security strategy requires a systematic approach that integrates technical controls, secure development practices, and continuous monitoring. Here's a step-by-step guide:

Step 1: Integrate Security into the SDLC

- **Design Phase:**
  Incorporate security requirements from the outset. Use threat modeling to identify potential risks and design countermeasures.

- **Development Phase:**
  Adopt secure coding practices and integrate SAST tools into your development environment. Educate developers on common vulnerabilities (e.g., those listed in the OWASP Top 10).

- **Testing Phase:**
  Implement DAST and penetration testing to validate the security of the application before deployment.

- **Deployment and Maintenance:**
  Use WAFs, RASP, and continuous monitoring to protect the application in production. Regularly update and patch the application to address newly discovered vulnerabilities.

Step 2: Establish Clear Policies and Standards

- **Secure Coding Standards:**
  Define coding standards and best practices that developers must follow.

- **Security Testing Policies:**
  Establish guidelines for regular static and dynamic testing, including mandatory penetration tests before major releases.

- **Incident Response:**
  Develop an application-specific incident response plan outlining steps to take if a security breach is detected.

Step 3: Deploy and Integrate Security Tools

- **SAST and DAST Tools:**
  Integrate these tools into your CI/CD pipeline to automate security testing.

- **WAF Deployment:**
  Configure a WAF to protect your web applications from common exploits.

- **RASP Solutions:**
  Consider deploying RASP to provide an additional layer of runtime protection.

Step 4: Continuous Monitoring and Improvement

- **Logging and SIEM Integration:**
  Collect logs from applications and integrate them with your SIEM system for real-time threat detection.

- **Regular Audits:**
  Conduct periodic security audits and vulnerability assessments to ensure compliance with policies.

- **Feedback Loop:**
  Use findings from security tests and incidents to update development practices and security policies continuously.

Step 5: Training and Awareness

- **Developer Training:**
  Regularly train developers on secure coding practices and emerging threats.

- **User Awareness:**
  Educate end-users on the importance of secure interactions with applications, such as avoiding suspicious downloads and recognizing phishing attempts.

- **Cross-Functional Workshops:**
  Organize sessions that bring together development, operations, and security teams to foster a collaborative culture of security.

Actionable Task

- **Secure Code Review Exercise:**
  Select a small module of your application and conduct a secure code review using a SAST tool. Identify at least three vulnerabilities and propose remediation strategies. Document the process and share your findings with your development team.

- **Policy Drafting Exercise:**
  Draft a sample security policy for web application development that includes guidelines on input validation, error handling, and use of encryption. Ensure that the policy addresses both development practices and post-deployment monitoring.

8.4 Real-World Applications and Case Studies

Case Study 1: Strengthening Web Application Security in a Financial Institution

A mid-sized bank recognized that its online banking platform was vulnerable to injection attacks and cross-site scripting (XSS). The bank implemented a comprehensive application security strategy:

- **Threat Modeling:**
  During the design phase, security teams mapped out potential attack vectors based on the OWASP Top 10 vulnerabilities.

- **SAST and DAST Integration:**
  Static and dynamic analysis tools were integrated into the development pipeline, catching vulnerabilities early.

- **WAF Deployment:**
  A WAF was deployed to filter malicious traffic before it reached the application.

- **Outcome:**
  The bank reported a 45% reduction in security incidents and increased customer confidence in the online platform.

Case Study 2: Implementing DevSecOps in a Global E-Commerce Company

A global e-commerce company faced challenges in maintaining security across frequent releases. The company adopted a DevSecOps approach:

- **Secure SDLC:**
  Security was embedded in every stage of the development lifecycle, with continuous testing using SAST and DAST tools.

- **Automation:**
  CI/CD pipelines were enhanced with automated security tests that prevented vulnerable code from reaching production.

- **RASP and Continuous Monitoring:**
  RASP was deployed to protect the application in real time, and logs were centralized in a SIEM system for ongoing monitoring.

- **Outcome:**
  The company achieved a 60% reduction in vulnerabilities, faster remediation times, and improved overall resilience, especially during high-traffic periods.

Global Insight:
A European technology firm integrated passwordless authentication into its application security strategy, reducing user friction while maintaining robust protection. This forward-thinking approach has set new industry standards for balancing usability and security.

8.5 Resources and Next Steps

To further enhance your application security expertise, consider the following resources:

- **Online Courses:**

  - Coursera, Udemy, and Cybrary offer specialized courses on secure coding, DevSecOps, and application security testing.

- **Books:**

  - *"The Web Application Hacker's Handbook"*

  - *"Secure Coding in C and C++"* for language-specific guidelines.

- **Certifications:**

  - Look into certifications such as Certified Secure Software Lifecycle Professional (CSSLP) or GIAC Web Application Penetration Tester (GWAPT).

- **Professional Organizations:**

  - Engage with (ISC)^2, ISACA, or OWASP chapters for networking and staying updated on best practices.

- **Tools:**

    - Experiment with open-source tools like OWASP ZAP for DAST and integrate SAST tools like SonarQube into your development process.

Practical Tip:
Start by integrating a SAST tool into your CI/CD pipeline. Monitor the results for a specific project and use the insights to refine your secure coding practices. Document your progress and share feedback with your team.

8.6 Chapter Takeaways

Key Points:

- **Application security** is vital for protecting software throughout its lifecycle, ensuring that vulnerabilities are detected and remediated early.

- Core components include **secure coding practices, SAST, DAST, penetration testing, WAFs, DevSecOps, and RASP.**

- Effective implementation requires integrating security into every stage of the SDLC, supported by continuous monitoring and regular audits.

- Real-world case studies demonstrate how structured application security measures can lead to significant reductions in vulnerabilities and improved compliance.

- Emerging trends, such as passwordless authentication and decentralized identity, are reshaping the future of application security.

8.7 Test Your Knowledge

1. **Which of the following best describes Static Application Security Testing (SAST)?**
   A. Testing applications during runtime for vulnerabilities
   B. Analyzing source code or binaries for vulnerabilities without executing the application
   C. Simulating attacks on a live application
   D. Monitoring network traffic for malicious activity

2. **What is the main purpose of a Web Application Firewall (WAF)?**
   A. To encrypt data at rest
   B. To filter and block malicious HTTP traffic
   C. To provide a single sign-on experience
   D. To monitor code quality

3. **Scenario Question:**
   Imagine you are responsible for securing a new customer portal for an online retailer. Describe one strategy you would implement to ensure the portal is secure from common vulnerabilities such as injection attacks and cross-site scripting. Include specific tools or methodologies that might be used in your approach.

4. **Reflective Exercise:**
   Identify two common vulnerabilities from the OWASP Top 10. For each, propose a mitigation strategy and explain how you would test its effectiveness. Also, outline how you would document and communicate these mitigation efforts to your development team.

8.8 Final Thoughts

Application security is an essential pillar of cyber defense that safeguards the software applications central to your business operations. By embedding security practices throughout the SDLC and leveraging advanced tools like SAST, DAST, WAFs, and RASP, organizations can proactively identify and remediate vulnerabilities before they are exploited. This chapter has provided you with a comprehensive guide to the core components, implementation strategies, and emerging trends in application security.

As you continue through this book, you will see how the principles discussed here integrate with other areas of cyber defense, forming a cohesive strategy that protects every layer of your digital environment. Implementing strong application security measures not only mitigates risk but also builds trust with users and stakeholders, paving the way for a secure and resilient future.

Thank you for exploring Chapter 8. Apply these insights and actionable tasks to enhance the security of your applications and continue your journey toward mastering cyber defense.

End of Chapter 8

Effective cyber defense requires a proactive approach to identifying threats, detecting anomalies, and responding rapidly to incidents. In this chapter, we explore the strategies, tools, and processes that underpin robust monitoring, detection, and response (MDR) systems. Building on the foundational concepts from previous chapters—risk management, network security, endpoint security, and IAM—we now focus on how to continuously watch over your digital environment, quickly detect threats, and respond effectively to minimize damage.

Expert Insight:
"In today's threat landscape, continuous monitoring and rapid response are the keys to staying one step ahead of attackers. It's not just about detecting a breach—it's about acting on that information immediately." — Senior Cybersecurity Analyst

9.1 What Is Monitoring, Detection, and Response?

Monitoring, Detection, and Response (MDR) is an integrated approach to cybersecurity that involves continuously observing systems for signs of malicious activity, identifying potential threats through real-time analytics, and responding promptly to contain and remediate incidents. Its primary objectives are to:

- **Monitor:** Maintain constant vigilance over network traffic, endpoints, and system logs.

- **Detect:** Identify anomalies and potential threats using advanced analytics and threat intelligence.

- **Respond:** Execute pre-defined procedures to mitigate incidents and recover systems, minimizing damage and downtime.

This integrated approach ensures that organizations can swiftly address security incidents before they escalate into major breaches.

9.2 Core Components of MDR

Modern MDR strategies rely on a variety of tools and technologies, each contributing to a layered defense. Key components include:

Security Information and Event Management (SIEM)

- **Purpose:** Aggregate and analyze logs from various sources—networks, endpoints, and applications—to detect anomalies.

- **Functionality:** Correlate events from disparate systems to provide a comprehensive view of the security landscape.

- **Example:** SIEM solutions like Splunk or IBM QRadar help security teams pinpoint unusual behavior that might indicate an attack.

Intrusion Detection and Prevention Systems (IDS/IPS)

- **Purpose:** Monitor network traffic to detect and, in the case of IPS, actively block malicious activities.

- **Types:**

  - **Network-based IDS/IPS:** Monitor network traffic in real-time.

  - **Host-based IDS/IPS:** Focus on activities on individual devices.

- **Benefit:** Early detection of threats prevents them from spreading further within the network.

Endpoint Detection and Response (EDR)

- **Purpose:** Provide continuous monitoring and response capabilities at the endpoint level.

- **Capabilities:** Detect sophisticated threats that evade traditional anti-virus solutions, collect forensic data, and support rapid incident response.

- **Tools:** Leading EDR solutions include CrowdStrike, SentinelOne, and Carbon Black.

Threat Intelligence Integration

- **Purpose:** Enhance detection capabilities by incorporating real-time threat intelligence feeds.

- **Functionality:** Use global data on attacker tactics, techniques, and procedures (TTPs) to update detection rules and prioritize alerts.

- **Outcome:** More accurate detection and faster response to emerging threats.

Anomaly Detection and Behavioral Analytics

- **Purpose:** Identify deviations from normal activity that may indicate a breach.

- **Methods:** Machine learning algorithms analyze historical data to detect unusual patterns.

- **Advantage:** Enables detection of novel threats that signature-based systems might miss.

Incident Response Platforms (IRP)

- **Purpose:** Coordinate and automate responses to security incidents.

- **Functionality:** Provide workflows for investigation, containment, and remediation, often integrating with SIEM and other security tools.

- **Example:** SOAR (Security Orchestration, Automation, and Response) platforms like Demisto or Phantom streamline incident response processes.

9.3 Implementing a Monitoring, Detection, and Response Strategy

A well-structured MDR strategy involves careful planning and integration of technologies, processes, and people. Here's a step-by-step guide to implementation:

Step 1: Define Critical Assets and Data Flows

- **Asset Inventory:**
  Identify and document all critical assets across networks, endpoints, and applications. This should

include hardware, software, data repositories, and communication channels.

- **Mapping Data Flows:**
Create diagrams that illustrate how data moves through your organization. Understanding these flows helps pinpoint potential vulnerabilities and critical monitoring points.

Step 2: Establish Baselines and Metrics

- **Baseline Activity:**
Determine what normal, expected behavior looks like by monitoring system performance and user activity over time. This baseline is crucial for detecting anomalies.

- **Key Performance Indicators (KPIs):**
Define metrics such as mean time to detect (MTTD) and mean time to respond (MTTR). These KPIs help measure the effectiveness of your MDR strategy.

Step 3: Deploy and Integrate Monitoring Tools

- **Implement SIEM Solutions:**
Integrate logs from firewalls, IDS/IPS, EDR, and other systems into a SIEM platform to facilitate real-time analysis and correlation.

- **Set Up IDS/IPS and EDR:**
Deploy IDS/IPS systems at critical network junctures and install EDR software on endpoints to continuously monitor for suspicious activity.

- **Integrate Threat Intelligence Feeds:**
  Connect your SIEM and IDS/IPS to threat intelligence sources to update detection rules dynamically.

- **Anomaly Detection Tools:**
  Use behavioral analytics tools to identify deviations from baseline activity.

Step 4: Develop an Incident Response Plan

- **Define Procedures:**
  Create detailed response protocols outlining steps to contain, investigate, and remediate incidents. Include escalation procedures and communication guidelines.

- **Team Coordination:**
  Establish roles and responsibilities for incident response, ensuring clear lines of communication among security, IT, and management teams.

- **Simulation and Drills:**
  Regularly conduct incident response exercises to test the plan's effectiveness and refine procedures based on lessons learned.

Step 5: Continuous Monitoring and Improvement

- **Regular Audits:**
  Periodically review and update your monitoring configurations and detection rules. Use post-incident analyses to identify areas for improvement.

- **Automated Alerts:**
  Configure automated alerts for high-priority anomalies and potential breaches.

- **Feedback Loop:**
  Integrate lessons learned from incidents and security assessments into your MDR strategy, ensuring continuous enhancement of your defenses.

Actionable Task

- **MDR Readiness Exercise:**
  Develop an inventory of critical assets and map data flows in your organization. Establish a baseline of normal network activity and identify three key indicators that would signal an anomaly. Using your SIEM platform, set up automated alerts for these indicators and document the expected response procedures. Share your findings with your incident response team for review and feedback.

- **Incident Response Drill:**
  Organize a simulated incident where a potential breach is detected. Run through your incident response plan and record the time taken to detect, respond, and remediate the incident. Identify any gaps in the process and propose improvements.

9.4 Real-World Applications and Case Studies

Case Study 1: Financial Institution's Proactive MDR Strategy

A mid-sized financial institution deployed a comprehensive MDR system to protect sensitive customer data and financial transactions:

- **Asset Mapping and Baselines:**
  The institution conducted a detailed inventory and established baseline behavior for network and user activity.

- **SIEM Integration:**
  Logs from firewalls, IDS/IPS, and EDR systems were centralized in a SIEM solution, enabling real-time threat detection.

- **Threat Intelligence:**
  Integration with global threat feeds allowed the institution to update detection rules dynamically.

- **Incident Response:**
  A well-practiced incident response plan reduced the mean time to detect (MTTD) by 30% and the mean time to respond (MTTR) by 40%.

- **Outcome:**
  The institution reported a 50% reduction in successful breach attempts and enhanced customer trust through improved security posture.

Case Study 2: Global E-Commerce Company Enhances MDR

A global e-commerce company needed to secure its extensive digital infrastructure, which spanned multiple data centers and cloud environments:

- **Continuous Monitoring:**
  The company deployed advanced SIEM and EDR solutions across its global operations to ensure 24/7 monitoring.

- **Anomaly Detection:**
  Behavioral analytics tools were used to detect deviations from established baselines, particularly during peak shopping periods.

- **Automated Incident Response:**
  SOAR platforms were integrated to automate routine responses, freeing up security analysts for more complex investigations.

- **Outcome:**
  The company achieved a 60% reduction in the impact of security incidents, with faster remediation times and improved compliance with international data protection regulations.

Global Insight:
A European retail firm integrated real-time monitoring with AI-driven anomaly detection, resulting in a 55% improvement in detection accuracy and setting a new benchmark for proactive threat management.

9.5 Resources and Next Steps

To further enhance your MDR capabilities, consider these resources:

- **Online Courses:**

  - Platforms like Coursera, Udemy, and Cybrary offer courses on SIEM, IDS/IPS, EDR, and incident response.

- **Books:**

  o *"The Practice of Network Security Monitoring"*

  o *"Incident Response & Computer Forensics"*

- **Certifications:**

  o Consider certifications such as Certified Incident Handler (GCIH) or Certified Information Systems Security Professional (CISSP) with a focus on incident response.

- **Professional Organizations:**

  o Engage with $(ISC)^2$, ISACA, and SANS Institute for training, networking, and the latest research on MDR.

- **Tools:**

  o Experiment with open-source SIEM platforms (e.g., ELK Stack) and IDS/IPS solutions to gain hands-on experience.

Practical Tip:
Begin by setting up a small-scale SIEM implementation to collect logs from key network devices and endpoints. Use this as a testing ground for refining your detection rules and alerting mechanisms.

9.6 Chapter Takeaways

Key Points:

- **Monitoring, Detection, and Response (MDR)** is an integrated approach that enables continuous oversight of your digital environment, quick identification of threats, and rapid incident response.

- Core components include **SIEM, IDS/IPS, EDR, threat intelligence, anomaly detection,** and **incident response platforms** such as SOAR.

- A systematic MDR strategy involves defining critical assets, establishing baselines, integrating diverse monitoring tools, and developing a robust incident response plan.

- Real-world case studies demonstrate that effective MDR can reduce detection and response times significantly, leading to a lower overall impact of security incidents.

- Continuous improvement and regular training are vital to keep pace with evolving threats.

9.7 Test Your Knowledge

1. **Which of the following is a primary function of a SIEM system in an MDR strategy?**
   A. Encrypting data in transit
   B. Aggregating and correlating logs from various sources to detect anomalies
   C. Blocking malicious traffic in real time
   D. Managing user access permissions

2. **What is the main benefit of integrating threat intelligence into your monitoring and detection systems?**
   A. Reducing the need for manual log reviews
   B. Automatically updating detection rules based on global threat data
   C. Increasing network speed
   D. Simplifying compliance reporting

3. **Scenario Question:**
   Imagine you are tasked with improving the incident response capabilities at a multinational corporation. Describe one strategy you would implement (e.g., automating incident response with a SOAR platform) and explain how it would help reduce the mean time to respond (MTTR) to security incidents. Include specific tools or methodologies in your answer.

4. **Reflective Exercise:**
   Draw a simplified network diagram of your organization, highlighting key monitoring points (e.g., where SIEM collects logs, IDS/IPS placements). Identify one potential weakness in your current setup and propose an enhancement. Explain how you would test and communicate this improvement to your team.

9.8 Final Thoughts

Monitoring, Detection, and Response is at the heart of a proactive cyber defense strategy. By continuously monitoring your systems, detecting anomalies in real-time, and responding swiftly to incidents, you can significantly reduce the risk and impact of cyber-attacks. This chapter has provided a detailed exploration of the tools, processes, and strategies essential for an effective MDR approach—from SIEM and IDS/IPS to EDR and automated incident response platforms.

As you move forward in this book, the MDR principles discussed here will integrate with other core areas, such as network security, endpoint security, and risk management, to form a comprehensive defense strategy. Continuous improvement, regular training, and a proactive mindset are key to staying ahead in today's rapidly evolving threat landscape.

Thank you for exploring Chapter 9. Apply these insights and actionable tasks to refine your monitoring and response capabilities and continue your journey toward mastering cyber defense.

End of Chapter 9

Incident Response and Recovery is the final, yet critical, component of a comprehensive cyber defense strategy. When preventive measures fail and an incident occurs, having a well-prepared response plan can mean the difference between a minor disruption and a full-blown crisis. In this chapter, we explore the principles, processes, and tools essential for managing security incidents and ensuring rapid recovery. Drawing on best practices such as those outlined in NIST SP 800-61, you will learn how to prepare, respond, and recover effectively from cyber-attacks while minimizing damage and restoring operations swiftly.

Expert Insight:
"An effective incident response strategy isn't just about reacting quickly—it's about learning from each incident to continually strengthen your defenses." — Incident Response Manager

10.1 What Is Incident Response and Recovery?

Incident Response (IR) is the process by which an organization prepares for, detects, and responds to cyber security incidents. Recovery, on the other hand, focuses on restoring systems and data to normal operations after an incident. Together, they form a lifecycle that ensures:

- **Preparation:** Establishing plans, policies, and procedures before an incident occurs.

- **Detection and Analysis:** Quickly identifying and understanding the scope and impact of an incident.

- **Containment:** Limiting the damage by isolating affected systems.

- **Eradication:** Removing the root cause and eliminating threats.

- **Recovery:** Restoring systems to full functionality and verifying that they are no longer compromised.

- **Post-Incident Review:** Learning from the incident to improve future response efforts.

By integrating these phases, organizations can not only mitigate damage but also build resilience against future threats.

10.2 Core Components of Incident Response

A robust Incident Response and Recovery strategy is built on several key components:

Incident Response Planning

- **Purpose:** Establish a documented plan that outlines the procedures to follow during a security incident.

- **Components:** Roles and responsibilities, communication protocols, escalation paths, and external contacts.

- **Standards:** Many organizations reference frameworks like NIST SP 800-61 for structuring their response plans.

Detection and Analysis

- **Detection Tools:** Utilize SIEM systems, intrusion detection systems (IDS), and endpoint detection and response (EDR) tools to identify anomalies.

- **Analysis:** Determine the nature, scope, and impact of the incident through forensic investigation and log analysis.

- **Key Metrics:** Mean Time to Detect (MTTD) is a critical measure for evaluating detection efficiency.

Containment Strategies

- **Short-Term Containment:** Actions taken immediately to limit the spread of the incident (e.g., isolating affected network segments).

- **Long-Term Containment:** Measures that allow continued business operations while preventing further compromise.

- **Goal:** Balance between minimizing damage and maintaining essential services.

Eradication and Recovery

- **Eradication:** Removing malware, closing vulnerabilities, and eliminating the root cause of the incident.

- **Recovery:** Restoring systems and data from backups, patching vulnerabilities, and validating system integrity.

- **Verification:** Ensure that systems are secure and function correctly before resuming normal operations.

Communication and Reporting

- **Internal Communication:** Clear, timely updates to management, IT teams, and relevant stakeholders.

- **External Communication:** Notifications to customers, regulators, or law enforcement as required by compliance standards.

- **Documentation:** Comprehensive incident reports that detail the incident's timeline, impact, and response actions.

Post-Incident Analysis (Lessons Learned)

- **Debrief:** Conduct a thorough review of the incident to identify what went well and areas for improvement.

- **Policy Updates:** Revise incident response plans, update security controls, and adjust training based on findings.

- **Continuous Improvement:** Integrate lessons learned to strengthen future incident response and overall security posture.

10.3 Implementing an Incident Response Plan

Building and deploying an effective Incident Response plan requires a systematic, multi-step approach:

Step 1: Preparation

- **Develop an Incident Response Policy:**
  Establish clear policies that outline roles, responsibilities, and procedures for incident handling.

Ensure that the policy aligns with industry standards such as NIST SP 800-61.

- **Form an Incident Response Team:**
  Designate a cross-functional team with members from IT, security, legal, and communications. Define clear roles for each team member.

- **Establish Communication Protocols:**
  Define internal and external communication channels, including escalation procedures and pre-approved messaging for public disclosures.

Step 2: Detection and Analysis

- **Deploy Monitoring Tools:**
  Integrate SIEM, IDS/IPS, and EDR solutions to provide continuous monitoring. Configure these tools to alert the incident response team upon detecting suspicious activities.

- **Define Baselines and KPIs:**
  Establish normal operating behavior to identify deviations. Key metrics such as MTTD help measure the effectiveness of your detection capabilities.

- **Incident Classification:**
  Develop criteria to categorize incidents by severity, helping determine the appropriate response level.

Step 3: Containment, Eradication, and Recovery

- **Short-Term Containment:**
  Immediately isolate affected systems to prevent further spread. For example, disconnect compromised devices from the network.

- **Long-Term Containment:**
  Implement measures that allow the business to continue operating while ensuring that the threat is neutralized.

- **Eradication:**
  Identify and remove the root cause, such as deleting malicious files or patching vulnerabilities.

- **Recovery:**
  Restore systems from backups, reinstall software as necessary, and verify that systems are secure before returning to normal operations.

- **Testing:**
  Validate that the recovered systems are fully operational and secure, using both manual testing and automated tools.

Step 4: Post-Incident Review

- **Debriefing:**
  Convene the incident response team to discuss the incident's handling, identifying successes and areas for improvement.

- **Documentation:**
  Compile a comprehensive incident report detailing timelines, actions taken, and lessons learned.

- **Policy Refinement:**
  Update incident response procedures and security policies based on the insights gained.

Actionable Task

- **Incident Response Drill:**
  Organize a simulated security incident to test your response plan. Document the entire process—from detection through recovery—and calculate your MTTD and MTTR. Identify any procedural gaps and propose improvements to your incident response plan.

- **Incident Report Template Exercise:**
  Draft an incident report template that includes sections for incident details, detection methods, containment actions, eradication efforts, recovery steps, and lessons learned. Share this template with your incident response team and solicit feedback to refine it.

10.4 Real-World Applications and Case Studies

Case Study 1: A Financial Institution's Rapid Response

A mid-sized financial institution faced a ransomware attack that encrypted critical customer data. Their response included:

- **Rapid Detection:**
  Integration of SIEM and EDR tools allowed them to detect the breach within minutes.

- **Containment:**
  Affected systems were isolated immediately to prevent lateral movement.

- **Eradication and Recovery:**
  The institution restored operations from encrypted backups and patched the exploited vulnerability.

- **Outcome:**
  The rapid response reduced downtime by 40%, and detailed post-incident analysis led to updated security protocols and improved threat detection capabilities.

Case Study 2: Global E-Commerce Incident Handling

A global e-commerce company experienced a data breach involving unauthorized access to customer information:

- **Detection and Analysis:**
  Behavioral analytics and anomaly detection within their SIEM flagged unusual access patterns.

- **Coordinated Response:**
  A well-documented incident response plan was executed, involving cross-functional teams to contain and eradicate the threat.

- **Post-Incident Review:**
  Detailed incident reports revealed areas for improvement in access control, leading to stricter IAM policies.

- **Outcome:**
  The company reduced its Mean Time to Respond (MTTR) by 35% and significantly improved customer trust through transparent communication and rapid remediation.

Global Insight:
A European telecommunications firm integrated automated incident response platforms (SOAR) with their SIEM, achieving a 50% faster response rate and setting a benchmark for proactive threat management in the region.

10.5 Resources and Next Steps

To further enhance your incident response and recovery capabilities, explore these resources:

- **Online Courses:**
  - Platforms like Coursera, Udemy, and Cybrary offer courses on incident response, digital forensics, and recovery strategies.

- **Books:**
  - *"NIST SP 800-61 – Computer Security Incident Handling Guide"*
  - *"Incident Response & Computer Forensics"*

- **Certifications:**
  - Consider certifications such as Certified Incident Handler (GCIH) or Certified Information Systems Security Professional (CISSP) with a focus on incident response.

- **Professional Organizations:**
  - Engage with SANS Institute, $(ISC)^2$, and ISACA for training, networking, and the latest research in incident response.

- **Tools:**
  - Experiment with open-source SIEM platforms (e.g., the ELK Stack), IDS/IPS solutions, and incident response tools to gain hands-on experience.

Practical Tip:
Begin by setting up an incident response simulation in a controlled environment. Use this simulation to refine your detection, containment, and recovery procedures, and document your findings for continuous improvement.

10.6 Chapter Takeaways

Key Points:

- **Incident Response and Recovery (IRR)** is a proactive, structured process to manage and mitigate security incidents, reducing damage and ensuring swift restoration of operations.

- The process includes **preparation, detection and analysis, containment, eradication, recovery,** and **post-incident review**.

- Core components such as **SIEM, IDS/IPS, EDR, threat intelligence,** and **SOAR platforms** are critical for effective monitoring, detection, and automated response.

- Real-world case studies demonstrate how a well-executed IRR strategy can significantly reduce downtime and improve overall security posture.

- Continuous improvement through regular training, audits, and updating of incident response plans is essential to adapt to evolving threats.

10.7 Test Your Knowledge

1. **Which phase of the incident response process focuses on isolating affected systems to prevent further spread?**
   A. Preparation
   B. Detection and Analysis
   C. Containment
   D. Recovery

2. **What does MTTR (Mean Time to Respond) measure in an incident response strategy?**
   A. The average time taken to detect an incident
   B. The average time taken to contain and remediate an incident
   C. The frequency of incidents over time
   D. The effectiveness of a SIEM system

3. **Scenario Question:**
   Imagine you are the incident response manager at a multinational corporation. You detect unusual login attempts using your SIEM system. Describe one strategy you would use to contain the incident and explain how you would coordinate your team to investigate and remediate the issue. Include specific tools or methodologies that might be used.

4. **Reflective Exercise:**
   Draw a simplified incident response flowchart outlining each phase of the process in your organization. Identify one potential gap in your current plan and propose an improvement. Explain how you would test and validate this enhancement, and how you would communicate the change to your stakeholders.

10.8 Final Thoughts

Incident Response and Recovery is not just a reactive process—it's a critical component of proactive cyber defense. By preparing thoroughly, detecting incidents swiftly, and responding effectively, organizations can minimize the impact of security breaches and maintain business continuity. This chapter has provided a detailed exploration of the key phases of incident response, the tools and strategies required for rapid remediation, and the importance of post-incident analysis for continuous improvement.

As you progress through this book, you'll see how the principles of Incident Response and Recovery integrate with other core areas such as risk management, network security, and endpoint security to form a cohesive, resilient defense strategy. Continuous monitoring, regular training, and a well-practiced incident response plan are essential to staying ahead in today's fast-evolving threat landscape.

Thank you for exploring Chapter 10. Apply these insights and actionable tasks to refine your incident response capabilities and continue your journey toward mastering cyber defense.

End of Chapter 10

Security awareness and human-centric defense represent the human side of cyber defense. Even the most advanced technological controls can be undermined by human error, social engineering, or simple lapses in judgment. This chapter focuses on cultivating a security-aware culture, educating users on cyber threats, and developing policies and practices that empower every individual to act as a first line of defense. Building on the technical strategies discussed in earlier chapters, we now shift our focus to the people and processes that fortify your organization's cybersecurity posture.

Expert Insight:
"Technology can only take you so far. Without a security-aware culture, even the best systems can be compromised by human error." — Chief Information Security Officer

11.1 What Is Security Awareness and Human-Centric Defense?

Security awareness involves educating and training individuals to recognize and respond appropriately to cyber threats. Human-centric defense extends this concept by designing policies, practices, and systems that account for human behavior. Together, they aim to:

- **Reduce Human Error:** Empower users with knowledge to avoid common pitfalls such as phishing scams and unsafe browsing.

- **Enhance Response:** Equip employees with the skills to report and respond to suspicious activity quickly.

- **Build a Security Culture:** Foster an environment where security is a shared responsibility and continuous learning is encouraged.

By focusing on these areas, organizations can transform every employee into a vigilant defender, reducing overall risk and complementing technical controls.

11.2 Core Components of Security Awareness

A successful security awareness program combines training, policies, and regular reinforcement. Key components include:

Training Programs

- **Purpose:** Provide comprehensive, ongoing education on cyber threats, best practices, and incident reporting.

- **Content:** Topics should include phishing recognition, secure password practices, safe use of social media, and the importance of software updates.

- **Methods:** Use interactive training sessions, online modules, and simulated phishing exercises to reinforce learning.

Awareness Campaigns

- **Internal Communications:** Regular newsletters, posters, and emails highlighting recent threats and security tips.

- **Gamification:** Incorporate games and competitions that reward good security practices, making learning engaging and memorable.

- **Real-World Examples:** Share anonymized case studies and recent incidents to illustrate the impact of security breaches and the importance of vigilance.

Policy and Procedures

- **Clear Guidelines:** Develop and disseminate security policies that define acceptable use, incident reporting, and response procedures.

- **User Accountability:** Establish protocols for reporting suspicious activities and ensure that policies are enforced consistently.

- **Periodic Reviews:** Regularly update policies to reflect emerging threats and lessons learned from incidents.

Human-Centric Design

- **User-Friendly Systems:** Design systems that incorporate security without impeding productivity. For example, streamlined Single Sign-On (SSO) and intuitive multi-factor authentication (MFA) processes.

- **Feedback Mechanisms:** Provide channels for employees to share feedback on security tools and policies, fostering continuous improvement.

- **Supportive Culture:** Encourage a culture where security is viewed as everyone's responsibility, not just the IT department's.

11.3 Implementing a Security Awareness Program

Implementing a comprehensive security awareness program requires careful planning, ongoing commitment, and measurable goals. Here's a structured approach:

Step 1: Assess the Current Security Culture

- **Surveys and Assessments:**
  Conduct surveys to gauge employees' current knowledge of cyber threats and security best practices.

- **Identify Gaps:**
  Use assessment results to identify areas where additional training is needed, such as phishing awareness or secure password management.

Step 2: Develop Tailored Training and Awareness Materials

- **Content Development:**
  Create training modules covering the fundamentals of cybersecurity, focusing on real-world scenarios relevant to your organization.

- **Interactive Exercises:**
  Develop simulated phishing tests, quizzes, and role-playing exercises to engage employees actively.

- **Multi-Channel Delivery:**
  Utilize a mix of in-person training sessions, online courses, and regular email updates to reach all employees.

Step 3: Establish Clear Security Policies and Procedures

- **Policy Creation:**
  Draft policies that detail acceptable use of systems, incident reporting protocols, and data handling procedures.

- **Communication:**
  Clearly communicate these policies through employee handbooks, internal portals, and periodic refresher sessions.

- **Enforcement:**
  Implement monitoring mechanisms to ensure policies are followed and provide feedback where necessary.

Step 4: Foster a Security-First Culture

- **Leadership Involvement:**
  Ensure that senior management actively participates in and endorses security initiatives. Their commitment reinforces the importance of security at every level.

- **Recognition and Rewards:**
  Create programs that recognize employees who exemplify good security practices. This can include awards, public recognition, or incentives.

- **Regular Updates and Drills:**
  Continuously update training materials based on the latest threats and conduct regular drills to keep security top of mind.

Step 5: Continuous Monitoring and Improvement

- **Feedback Loops:**
  Collect feedback through surveys and direct

communication to understand what works and what needs improvement.

- **Metrics and KPIs:**
  Establish key performance indicators such as reduced phishing click rates, improved incident reporting times, and increased participation in training programs.

- **Iterative Improvements:**
  Use the collected data to refine training content, update policies, and adjust awareness campaigns.

Actionable Task

- **Security Awareness Inventory:**
  Conduct a survey among employees to assess their current understanding of common cyber threats. Identify two areas where awareness is lacking and develop a mini-training session focused on these topics.

- **Phishing Simulation Exercise:**
  Launch a simulated phishing campaign to test the organization's response. Analyze the results to identify vulnerable groups, then plan targeted training to address these weaknesses. Document the process and share the results with management for further action.

11.4 Real-World Applications and Case Studies

Case Study 1: Financial Institution Enhances Security Awareness

A mid-sized bank, facing repeated phishing attacks, overhauled its security awareness program:

- **Training Initiative:**
  The bank implemented monthly interactive training sessions and simulated phishing campaigns. Over six months, phishing click rates dropped by 65%.

- **Policy Updates:**
  New policies were introduced to mandate the use of MFA and secure password practices, with regular reminders and rewards for compliance.

- **Outcome:**
  The combined efforts resulted in a 40% reduction in security incidents related to human error, significantly bolstering the bank's overall cyber defense posture.

Case Study 2: Global Retail Chain Builds a Culture of Security

A global retail chain recognized that its decentralized workforce was vulnerable to cyber threats due to inconsistent security practices:

- **Awareness Campaign:**
  A comprehensive awareness campaign was launched, including interactive webinars, gamified training, and real-time updates on emerging threats.

- **Employee Engagement:**
  Regular quizzes and competitions encouraged active participation, while an internal portal provided resources and best practices.

- **Outcome:**
  The initiative led to improved security behavior across the organization, with a 50% reduction in security breaches attributed to human error, and increased

confidence in the company's ability to safeguard customer data.

Global Insight:
An international technology firm integrated security awareness with its daily operations by embedding security tips into its intranet and conducting quarterly security drills. This proactive approach reduced incident response times by 30% and set a new industry standard for human-centric defense.

11.5 Resources and Next Steps

To further enhance your security awareness and human-centric defense capabilities, consider the following resources:

- **Online Courses:**

  o Coursera, Udemy, and Cybrary offer courses on security awareness, social engineering, and behavioral cybersecurity.

- **Books:**

  o *"Cybersecurity Awareness: A Practical Guide"*

  o *"The Human Factor in Cybersecurity"*

- **Certifications:**

  o Explore certifications such as Certified Information Systems Security Professional (CISSP) with a focus on human factors, or specialized courses in security awareness.

- **Professional Organizations:**

  - Engage with ISACA, (ISC)^2, and the SANS Institute for training, webinars, and workshops focused on human-centric security.

- **Tools:**

  - Experiment with phishing simulation tools and security awareness platforms that offer analytics and reporting.

Practical Tip:
Launch a pilot security awareness program in a small department first. Use this pilot to refine your training materials and strategies before rolling out the program organization-wide.

11.6 Chapter Takeaways

Key Points:

- **Security awareness and human-centric defense** focus on educating and empowering individuals to act as the first line of defense against cyber threats.

- Core components include **training programs, awareness campaigns, clear policies, and user-friendly systems.**

- Implementing an effective program involves assessing current knowledge, developing targeted training, establishing robust policies, and continuously monitoring and updating practices.

- Real-world case studies show that well-executed security awareness initiatives can significantly reduce incidents caused by human error.

- Emerging trends in human-centric defense include leveraging behavioral analytics and integrating security tips into everyday workflows.

11.7 Test Your Knowledge

1. **Which of the following best describes the purpose of security awareness training?**
   A. To deploy advanced technical controls
   B. To educate employees on recognizing and responding to cyber threats
   C. To develop encryption algorithms
   D. To automate network security tasks

2. **What is the main benefit of conducting simulated phishing exercises?**
   A. To test the effectiveness of encryption protocols
   B. To evaluate and improve employees' ability to detect phishing attempts
   C. To reduce the number of security policies
   D. To automate incident response

3. **Scenario Question:**
   Imagine you are tasked with improving security awareness in a multinational organization. Describe one strategy you would implement to educate employees about social engineering threats and explain how you would measure the effectiveness of this strategy. Include specific tools or methodologies that might be used.

135

4. **Reflective Exercise:**
   List two common security risks caused by human error
   (e.g., weak passwords, falling for phishing scams). For
   each risk, propose a mitigation strategy and outline
   how you would communicate the importance of these
   measures to non-technical stakeholders.

11.8 Final Thoughts

Security awareness and human-centric defense are essential
for a comprehensive cyber defense strategy. While technology
can mitigate many risks, it is ultimately the human element that
often represents the weakest link—and, when properly
empowered, the strongest defense. By educating employees,
fostering a culture of security, and integrating continuous
training and awareness into daily operations, organizations can
reduce vulnerabilities and respond more effectively to threats.

This chapter has provided a detailed exploration of security
awareness initiatives, key components, and implementation
strategies. The real-world case studies demonstrate that well-
designed programs can lead to significant improvements in
security behavior and incident reduction. As you progress
through this book, the human-centric principles discussed here
will complement technical controls to form a holistic and
resilient cyber defense framework.

Thank you for exploring Chapter 11. Apply these insights and
actionable tasks to build a robust security awareness program
and continue your journey toward mastering cyber defense.

End of Chapter 11

Cloud and hybrid environments have revolutionized the way organizations store and process data. However, this flexibility also introduces new security challenges that require specialized strategies. In this chapter, we explore the core principles, technologies, and best practices for securing cloud and hybrid environments. Building on the frameworks, risk management, network security, and endpoint security concepts discussed earlier, you will learn how to protect data, applications, and services in public, private, and hybrid cloud settings. Real-world case studies and actionable tasks illustrate how to apply these strategies effectively.

Expert Insight:
"Cloud security is a shared responsibility model—while providers secure the infrastructure, organizations must ensure their applications and data are protected. A strong cloud security strategy must address both aspects." — Cloud Security Architect

---

12.1 What Is Cloud and Hybrid Environment Security?

Cloud security involves protecting data, applications, and infrastructures hosted on cloud platforms from cyber threats. Hybrid security extends these principles to environments where on-premise systems and cloud services coexist. Key objectives include:

- **Confidentiality:** Ensuring that data in the cloud remains accessible only to authorized users.

- **Integrity:** Preventing unauthorized alterations to data and configurations.

- **Availability:** Guaranteeing that cloud services and applications are accessible when needed.

Security in cloud environments is governed by a shared responsibility model, where the cloud provider secures the underlying infrastructure, and the organization is responsible for securing data, applications, and user access.

12.2 Core Components of Cloud and Hybrid Environment Security

Securing cloud and hybrid environments requires a multi-layered approach that encompasses several critical components:

Shared Responsibility Model

- **Concept:**
  Understand that cloud security is divided between the provider and the customer. The provider secures the infrastructure (physical servers, storage, networking), while the customer is responsible for securing data, applications, and access controls.

- **Importance:**
  This model clarifies roles and helps organizations allocate resources effectively.

Cloud Security Posture Management (CSPM)

- **Purpose:**
  CSPM tools continuously monitor cloud configurations

to ensure they meet security best practices and compliance requirements.

- **Functionality:**
  They automatically detect misconfigurations, enforce policies, and provide remediation guidance.

- **Example:**
  CSPM solutions can alert you if a cloud storage bucket is publicly accessible.

Cloud Access Security Broker (CASB)

- **Purpose:**
  CASBs act as intermediaries between cloud service users and providers, enforcing security policies across cloud applications.

- **Capabilities:**
  They provide visibility into cloud usage, enforce data security policies, and protect against threats like data leakage and unauthorized access.

Encryption and Key Management

- **Data Encryption:**
  Encrypt data at rest and in transit using robust algorithms such as AES-256.

- **Key Management:**
  Use dedicated key management services (KMS) to control access to encryption keys.

- **Cloud Integration:**
  Many cloud providers offer integrated KMS solutions that streamline encryption processes.

Identity and Access Management (IAM) in the Cloud

- **Cloud IAM:**
  Extend IAM principles to cloud environments by managing user identities and access to cloud resources.

- **Single Sign-On (SSO) and MFA:**
  Implement SSO and multi-factor authentication to ensure secure access to cloud applications.

- **Federated Identity:**
  Use federated identity solutions to manage access across multiple cloud services seamlessly.

Network Security in the Cloud

- **Virtual Private Cloud (VPC):**
  Configure VPCs to isolate cloud resources and control network traffic.

- **Security Groups and Network ACLs:**
  Use these built-in firewalls to manage inbound and outbound traffic at the instance level.

- **Hybrid Connectivity:**
  Secure connections between on-premise networks and cloud environments using VPNs or dedicated links.

Monitoring and Compliance Tools

- **Log Management:**
  Collect and analyze logs from cloud resources using SIEM systems for real-time threat detection.

- **Compliance Automation:**
  Tools that continuously audit cloud configurations

against standards such as GDPR, HIPAA, or PCI-DSS help maintain compliance and reduce risk.

12.3 Implementing Cloud and Hybrid Environment Security

Deploying a robust cloud security strategy involves careful planning and integration of technology, processes, and policies. Follow these steps to secure your cloud and hybrid environments effectively:

Step 1: Assess and Inventory

- **Asset Inventory:**
  Identify all cloud assets and services in use, including public, private, and hybrid components.

- **Data Mapping:**
  Map data flows between on-premise systems and cloud environments to understand potential exposure.

- **Risk Assessment:**
  Evaluate risks associated with each asset, considering the shared responsibility model.

Step 2: Develop Cloud Security Policies

- **Define Roles and Responsibilities:**
  Clearly outline what security tasks are managed by the cloud provider and what must be managed internally.

- **Access and Data Protection Policies:**
  Develop policies for data encryption, IAM, and CASB use. Include guidelines for acceptable use and data handling.

- **Compliance Requirements:**
  Ensure policies align with relevant regulations and industry standards.

Step 3: Deploy Security Technologies

- **Implement CSPM and CASB:**
  Deploy CSPM tools to continuously monitor cloud configurations and CASBs to enforce security policies across cloud services.

- **Encryption and Key Management:**
  Utilize cloud provider KMS for managing encryption keys and enforce encryption on all sensitive data.

- **Secure Network Configurations:**
  Configure VPCs, security groups, and network ACLs to control traffic. Set up secure hybrid connections (e.g., VPNs) for integrated environments.

- **Extend IAM to Cloud:**
  Integrate cloud IAM solutions with existing directory services to ensure seamless and secure access management.

Step 4: Continuous Monitoring and Auditing

- **Real-Time Monitoring:**
  Use SIEM tools to collect logs from cloud resources, monitoring for anomalies and unauthorized access.

- **Compliance Checks:**
  Regularly audit cloud configurations against established policies and compliance frameworks.

- **Automated Alerts:**
  Set up alerts for configuration changes, access anomalies, or policy violations.

Step 5: Training and Awareness

- **Cloud Security Training:**
  Provide specialized training on cloud security best practices, emphasizing the shared responsibility model and proper configuration.

- **User Education:**
  Educate employees about the risks of misconfigured cloud services and the importance of following security protocols.

- **Ongoing Drills:**
  Regularly conduct simulated cloud security incidents to test response procedures and improve readiness.

Actionable Task

- **Cloud Security Assessment Exercise:**
  Conduct an inventory of all cloud assets and map out data flows between on-premise and cloud environments. Identify one critical asset and assess its security posture using a CSPM tool. Draft a plan outlining steps to remediate any misconfigurations or vulnerabilities, and schedule regular reviews of this plan.

- **Policy Drafting Exercise:**
  Draft a cloud security policy that specifies roles, responsibilities, and technical controls (e.g., encryption standards, IAM integration). Include a section on hybrid connectivity, ensuring secure communication

between on-premise systems and the cloud. Share the draft with your IT and compliance teams for feedback.

12.4 Real-World Applications and Case Studies

Case Study 1: Securing a Financial Institution's Cloud Infrastructure

A mid-sized financial institution migrated its critical applications to a public cloud while maintaining legacy systems on-premise. Their approach included:

- **CSPM Deployment:**
  Continuous monitoring of cloud configurations helped detect misconfigured storage buckets and insecure network settings.

- **Hybrid Network Security:**
  Secure VPN tunnels and VPC configurations were established to protect data flows between on-premise systems and the cloud.

- **IAM Extension:**
  Cloud IAM policies were integrated with the institution's existing Active Directory, ensuring consistent access controls.

- **Outcome:**
  The institution reduced configuration-related vulnerabilities by 55% and maintained regulatory compliance, boosting both customer confidence and operational efficiency.

Case Study 2: Global E-Commerce Cloud Security Enhancement

A global e-commerce company faced challenges managing security across multiple cloud platforms and hybrid environments:

- **CASB Integration:**
  CASB tools were deployed to monitor and enforce security policies across various cloud services, preventing data leakage.

- **Encryption and Key Management:**
  All sensitive customer data was encrypted at rest and in transit using AES-256, with keys managed through an integrated KMS.

- **Automated Compliance Audits:**
  Regular automated audits ensured that the company met international data protection standards such as GDPR.

- **Outcome:**
  The company achieved a 60% reduction in cloud misconfigurations and significantly improved its ability to detect and respond to cloud-related security incidents.

Global Insight:
A European telecommunications firm successfully implemented a hybrid cloud strategy by combining CSPM, CASB, and robust IAM policies. This integrated approach reduced security incidents by 50% and set a new standard for cloud security in highly regulated environments.

12.5 Resources and Next Steps

To deepen your expertise in cloud and hybrid environment security, consider these resources:

- **Online Courses:**

  - Coursera, Udemy, and Cybrary offer courses on cloud security fundamentals, CSPM, CASB, and hybrid cloud management.

- **Books:**

  - *"Cloud Security and Privacy"* by Tim Mather

  - *"Architecting Cloud Computing Solutions"* for practical insights into hybrid cloud security.

- **Certifications:**

  - Consider certifications such as Certified Cloud Security Professional (CCSP) or AWS Certified Security – Specialty.

- **Professional Organizations:**

  - Engage with Cloud Security Alliance (CSA), ISACA, and (ISC)^2 for training, networking, and updates on cloud security best practices.

- **Tools:**

  - Experiment with open-source CSPM tools, CASB trial versions, or cloud provider security dashboards (e.g., AWS Security Hub, Azure Security Center).

Practical Tip:
Begin by reviewing your current cloud configurations and conduct a CSPM assessment. Use the insights to update your security policies and integrate automated compliance checks. Document the changes and establish a regular review schedule.

12.6 Chapter Takeaways

Key Points:

- **Cloud and Hybrid Environment Security** focuses on protecting data, applications, and services hosted in cloud environments, as well as securing the integration between on-premise and cloud systems.

- Key components include the **shared responsibility model, CSPM, CASB, encryption and key management, cloud IAM, secure network configurations,** and **continuous monitoring.**

- A robust strategy involves a systematic approach: inventory and risk assessment, policy development, deployment of security controls, continuous monitoring, and regular training.

- Real-world case studies demonstrate significant improvements in security posture and compliance through the effective implementation of cloud security measures.

- Emerging trends such as multi-cloud strategies, passwordless access, and automated compliance are shaping the future of cloud security.

12.7 Test Your Knowledge

1. **Which of the following best describes the shared responsibility model in cloud security?**
   A. The cloud provider secures everything, and the customer is not responsible for security
   B. The customer is responsible for all aspects of security in the cloud
   C. The cloud provider secures the infrastructure, while the customer secures data, applications, and user access
   D. Security responsibilities are entirely outsourced to a third-party vendor

2. **What is the primary function of a Cloud Security Posture Management (CSPM) tool?**
   A. To encrypt data at rest
   B. To continuously monitor and enforce security configurations in cloud environments
   C. To provide single sign-on capabilities
   D. To manage user roles and permissions

3. **Scenario Question:**
   Imagine you are the cloud security manager for a multinational organization that uses a hybrid cloud strategy. Describe one specific strategy you would implement to secure data flows between on-premise systems and the cloud and explain how you would measure its effectiveness. Include references to tools or methodologies where appropriate.

4. **Reflective Exercise:**
   Create a basic diagram of your organization's cloud and hybrid network architecture. Identify key assets and potential vulnerabilities and propose one security

improvement for each. Then, outline how you would update your security policies to reflect these improvements and communicate the changes to both technical and non-technical stakeholders.

12.8 Final Thoughts

Cloud and hybrid environment security is essential for protecting modern digital infrastructures. By leveraging the shared responsibility model, deploying advanced monitoring tools like CSPM and CASB, and integrating robust IAM and encryption practices, organizations can secure their cloud assets and ensure seamless, secure connectivity between on-premise and cloud systems. This chapter has provided a detailed exploration of the strategies and technologies that underpin effective cloud security, reinforced by real-world case studies and actionable tasks.

As you continue your journey through this book, the principles discussed here will integrate with other core areas—such as risk management, network security, and endpoint security—to form a comprehensive, layered defense strategy. Continuous monitoring, regular policy reviews, and proactive training are key to staying ahead in an ever-evolving threat landscape.

Thank you for exploring Chapter 12. Apply these insights and tasks to strengthen your cloud and hybrid security posture and continue your journey toward mastering cyber defense.

End of Chapter 12

Part 3: Advanced Topics and Emerging Trends

Chapter 13: Offensive Security (Ethical Hacking)

Offensive security, often referred to as ethical hacking, is a proactive approach that simulates cyber-attacks to identify vulnerabilities before malicious hackers can exploit them. In this chapter, we delve into the principles and practices of offensive security, exploring how ethical hackers use a variety of tools and techniques to assess and strengthen an organization's defenses. Positioned under Advanced Topics and Emerging Trends, this chapter builds on the foundational elements of risk management, network security, and endpoint security to show you how to think like an attacker—and, in turn, better defend against them.

Expert Insight:
"Ethical hacking is about understanding the enemy. By simulating real-world attacks, organizations can discover hidden vulnerabilities and take steps to neutralize them before they are exploited by criminals." — Lead Penetration Tester

---

13.1 What Is Offensive Security?

Offensive security encompasses the methods and practices used to simulate cyber-attacks in order to identify vulnerabilities in systems, networks, and applications. Also known as ethical hacking, it involves using the same tools, techniques, and processes as malicious hackers—but with authorization—to uncover security weaknesses. The primary goals are to:

- **Identify Vulnerabilities:** Discover potential security gaps before they are exploited.

- **Test Defenses:** Evaluate the effectiveness of existing security controls.

- **Enhance Resilience:** Provide actionable insights for remediation, thereby strengthening overall security posture.

Offensive security is not only a testing methodology; it is a critical component of a continuous improvement cycle that informs risk management, incident response, and strategic planning.

13.2 Core Components of Offensive Security

A comprehensive offensive security strategy consists of multiple layers and methodologies. Here are the key components:

Penetration Testing

- **Definition:**
  A simulated cyber-attack against your systems, designed to evaluate their security posture.

- **Types:**

  o **External Penetration Testing:** Focuses on internet-facing assets.

- o **Internal Penetration Testing:** Assesses risks from insiders or compromised internal devices.

- **Tools:**
Common tools include Metasploit, Burp Suite, and Nmap.

- **Outcome:**
Identification of exploitable vulnerabilities and a prioritized list of remediation actions.

Red Teaming

- **Definition:**
A comprehensive, adversary-simulated exercise that tests not just technology but also people and processes.

- **Scope:**
Involves multi-vector attacks that mimic real-world adversaries.

- **Benefit:**
Provides a holistic assessment of security readiness and incident response effectiveness.

- **Approach:**
Unlike targeted penetration tests, red team exercises are often longer, more dynamic engagements that simulate full-scale attacks.

Vulnerability Assessment

- **Definition:**
A systematic review of security weaknesses in an organization's systems.

- **Tools:**
  Vulnerability scanners like Nessus, Qualys, or OpenVAS.

- **Process:**
  Identifies vulnerabilities and categorizes them based on severity, but without exploiting them.

- **Integration:**
  Often used as a preliminary step before more targeted penetration tests.

Social Engineering

- **Definition:**
  Techniques that exploit human behavior to gain unauthorized access.

- **Methods:**
  Phishing, pretexting, baiting, and tailgating are common examples.

- **Purpose:**
  Assess how well employees can recognize and resist manipulation, highlighting areas for improved training.

- **Outcome:**
  Insights that can drive more effective security awareness programs.

Exploit Development

- **Definition:**
  The process of identifying and creating tools to exploit discovered vulnerabilities.

- **Purpose:**
  Understand how vulnerabilities can be weaponized.

- **Use:**
  Often used by advanced ethical hackers to simulate sophisticated attacks and demonstrate potential impacts.

- **Ethical Considerations:**
  Must be conducted in controlled environments to avoid unintended damage.

13.3 Implementing Offensive Security

Deploying an offensive security program requires careful planning, clear policies, and integration with overall risk management and defensive strategies. Here's a step-by-step guide:

Step 1: Define Objectives and Scope

- **Set Clear Goals:**
  Determine what you want to achieve—whether it's identifying vulnerabilities, testing incident response, or evaluating user awareness.

- **Scope Determination:**
  Identify which systems, networks, and applications will be tested. Decide whether to include both external and internal assets.

- **Legal and Ethical Considerations:**
  Obtain the necessary permissions and define rules of engagement to ensure that all activities are authorized and controlled.

Step 2: Develop a Comprehensive Plan

- **Methodologies and Tools:**
  Decide on the types of tests (penetration testing, red teaming, vulnerability assessments) and the tools you will use.

- **Team Formation:**
  Assemble a team of ethical hackers with diverse skills. Consider engaging external experts if needed.

- **Timeline and Milestones:**
  Establish a realistic timeline for each phase of the testing process, including pre-testing planning, actual testing, and post-testing analysis.

Step 3: Execute Testing and Assess Vulnerabilities

- **Conduct Vulnerability Assessments:**
  Use automated tools to scan systems for known vulnerabilities.

- **Perform Penetration Testing:**
  Attempt to exploit vulnerabilities to understand their impact. Document each step carefully.

- **Red Team Exercises:**
  Simulate complex, multi-vector attacks to test the overall resilience of your security defenses.

- **Social Engineering Tests:**
  Evaluate employee readiness by simulating phishing attacks or other social engineering techniques.

Step 4: Analyze Findings and Remediate

- **Document Vulnerabilities:**
  Create a detailed report that outlines the vulnerabilities discovered, the methods used to exploit them, and their potential impact.

- **Prioritize Remediation:**
  Use risk assessment metrics, such as severity scores and potential business impact, to prioritize remediation efforts.

- **Implement Fixes:**
  Work with IT and development teams to address vulnerabilities through patching, configuration changes, or enhanced security controls.

- **Re-test:**
  Verify that remediation efforts have successfully mitigated the identified vulnerabilities.

Step 5: Continuous Improvement and Integration

- **Feedback Loop:**
  Incorporate lessons learned into your overall risk management and defensive strategies.

- **Regular Testing:**
  Schedule periodic testing to ensure that security controls remain effective against evolving threats.

- **Training and Awareness:**
  Use insights from offensive security tests to inform security awareness programs and improve employee resilience against social engineering.

Actionable Task

- **Ethical Hacking Simulation:**
  Organize a controlled penetration test of a non-critical system. Use a vulnerability scanner to identify potential weaknesses, then attempt to exploit these vulnerabilities using tools like Metasploit or Burp Suite. Document each step, measure the time taken for detection and remediation, and compile a detailed report with your findings. Share this report with your security team to drive continuous improvements.

- **Policy Drafting Exercise:**
  Create a draft policy outlining the rules and procedures for offensive security testing. Include guidelines on scope, permissions, and reporting. Ensure that the policy addresses legal and ethical considerations and is reviewed by both legal and IT teams.

13.4 Real-World Applications and Case Studies

Case Study 1: Financial Institution Penetration Testing

A mid-sized bank implemented regular penetration tests to strengthen its defenses:

- **Testing Scope:**
  The bank's external and internal networks, as well as its web applications, were subjected to comprehensive penetration testing.

- **Methodology:**
  Using automated tools and manual techniques, the tests

uncovered vulnerabilities in outdated software and misconfigured network services.

- **Remediation:**
  The bank prioritized fixes based on risk impact, patched software vulnerabilities, and tightened network configurations.

- **Outcome:**
  The initiative resulted in a 45% reduction in potential entry points for attackers and a significant improvement in regulatory compliance.

Case Study 2: Red Team Engagement in a Global E-Commerce Company

A global e-commerce company deployed a red team to simulate a real-world cyber-attack:

- **Exercise Design:**
  The red team used a mix of penetration testing, social engineering, and exploit development to mimic an advanced threat.

- **Findings:**
  The exercise revealed gaps in the company's incident response procedures and weaknesses in user awareness.

- **Improvements:**
  The company revised its incident response plan, enhanced employee training programs, and implemented additional technical controls.

- **Outcome:**
  The red team engagement led to a 60% improvement in

the company's incident detection and response times, along with a higher level of overall security maturity.

Global Insight:
A European financial services firm integrated advanced red teaming with continuous vulnerability assessments. By simulating attacks across multiple vectors, they achieved a 50% improvement in proactive threat identification, setting a benchmark for offensive security practices in their industry.

13.5 Resources and Next Steps

To expand your knowledge and practical skills in offensive security, consider these resources:

- **Online Courses:**

    - Platforms like Coursera, Udemy, and Cybrary offer courses on ethical hacking, penetration testing, and red team operations.

- **Books:**

    - *"The Web Application Hacker's Handbook"*

    - *"Hacking: The Art of Exploitation"*

- **Certifications:**

    - Certifications such as Certified Ethical Hacker (CEH), Offensive Security Certified Professional (OSCP), or GIAC Penetration Tester (GPEN) provide valuable credentials.

- **Professional Organizations:**

- o Engage with the EC-Council, Offensive Security, and ISACA for networking, training, and industry insights.

- **Tools:**

  - o Experiment with open-source tools like Metasploit, Burp Suite, Nmap, and OWASP ZAP to gain hands-on experience.

- **Workshops and Conferences:**

  - o Attend industry events such as DEF CON, Black Hat, or local hacking workshops to stay updated on the latest offensive security trends.

Practical Tip:
Begin by setting up a home lab environment where you can safely practice penetration testing and red teaming techniques. Use virtual machines to simulate a network, and apply the tools and techniques discussed in this chapter to build your skills.

13.6 Chapter Takeaways

Key Points:

- **Offensive Security (Ethical Hacking)** involves proactively testing systems to uncover vulnerabilities before attackers can exploit them.

- Core components include **penetration testing, red teaming, vulnerability assessments, social engineering,** and **exploit development**.

- A structured approach to offensive security involves defining clear objectives, developing a comprehensive testing plan, executing tests, and integrating the findings into your overall security strategy.

- Real-world case studies illustrate that regular offensive security testing can significantly reduce vulnerabilities and enhance an organization's ability to detect and respond to threats.

- Continuous learning and adaptation—along with emerging trends such as passwordless authentication—are essential for staying ahead in the evolving threat landscape.

13.7 Test Your Knowledge

1. **Which of the following best describes the purpose of penetration testing in offensive security?**
   A. To automate network monitoring
   B. To simulate cyber-attacks and identify vulnerabilities
   C. To encrypt sensitive data
   D. To manage user access

2. **What is the primary difference between penetration testing and red teaming?**
   A. Penetration testing is automated, while red teaming is manual
   B. Penetration testing focuses on technical vulnerabilities, while red teaming simulates multi-vector, real-world attack scenarios
   C. Red teaming only involves social engineering
   D. Penetration testing is only for web applications

3. **Scenario Question:**
   Imagine you are an ethical hacker engaged by a multinational corporation. You are tasked with performing a red team exercise that includes both technical and social engineering elements. Describe one specific technique you would use to test the organization's defenses and explain how you would document and report your findings to help improve their security posture.

4. **Reflective Exercise:**
   Identify two common vulnerabilities found during offensive security assessments (e.g., SQL injection, insecure configurations). For each vulnerability, propose one mitigation strategy and explain how you would test its effectiveness. Then, outline how you would communicate these findings to both technical and non-technical stakeholders.

13.8 Final Thoughts

Offensive security is an essential aspect of a comprehensive cyber defense strategy. By adopting ethical hacking practices, organizations can proactively identify and remediate vulnerabilities, thereby reducing the risk of successful attacks. This chapter has provided a detailed exploration of the methodologies, tools, and processes involved in offensive security—from penetration testing and red teaming to social engineering and exploit development. The real-world case studies and actionable tasks presented here demonstrate the tangible benefits of a proactive, offensive approach.

As you continue through this book, the offensive security principles discussed in this chapter will complement other core areas such as risk management, network security, and incident response. Embracing offensive security not only sharpens your defensive capabilities but also fosters a culture of continuous improvement and innovation.

Thank you for exploring Chapter 13. Apply these insights and practical exercises to build your offensive security skills and continue your journey toward mastering cyber defense.

End of Chapter 13

Cyber Threat Intelligence (CTI) is an essential discipline in modern cyber defense, transforming raw data into actionable insights about emerging threats. By analyzing adversary tactics, techniques, and procedures (TTPs), CTI enables organizations to anticipate and preempt potential attacks. In this chapter, we delve into the core concepts of CTI, its key components, and the methodologies for implementing effective threat intelligence programs. Building on earlier chapters covering risk management, network security, and incident response, you will learn how CTI empowers proactive defense and supports informed decision-making in today's dynamic threat landscape.

Expert Insight:
"Cyber threat intelligence is about turning data into foresight. It provides the context necessary to prioritize defenses and shape an organization's security posture against evolving adversaries." — Senior Threat Intelligence Analyst

14.1 What Is Cyber Threat Intelligence?

Cyber Threat Intelligence involves the systematic collection, analysis, and dissemination of information regarding potential or active cyber threats. The primary objectives of CTI are to:

- **Identify Threat Actors:** Understand who the attackers are, their motivations, and capabilities.

- **Analyze Attack Patterns:** Examine TTPs to predict future actions.

- **Inform Defensive Strategies:** Provide actionable insights that shape proactive security measures.

- **Enhance Incident Response:** Support faster and more effective responses when incidents occur.

CTI turns vast amounts of raw data—collected from internal logs, external threat feeds, and open-source intelligence (OSINT)—into strategic insights. These insights help organizations mitigate risks, tailor their defenses, and make informed decisions regarding security investments.

14.2 Core Components of Cyber Threat Intelligence

An effective CTI program relies on several key components that work together to provide a comprehensive picture of the threat landscape:

Data Collection and Aggregation

- **Internal Sources:**
  Data from SIEM systems, IDS/IPS, and endpoint detection tools provide insights into internal network activity.

- **External Sources:**
  Threat feeds, OSINT, dark web monitoring, and vendor intelligence reports contribute to the external threat landscape.

- **Aggregation Tools:**
  Platforms that consolidate and normalize data from various sources are essential for comprehensive analysis.

Analysis and Contextualization

- **Threat Analysis:**
  Analysts review the collected data to identify patterns, trends, and indicators of compromise (IOCs).

- **Tactics, Techniques, and Procedures (TTPs):**
  Understanding adversary methods helps predict potential future attacks.

- **Contextualization:**
  Intelligence is enriched with context such as geopolitical events, industry-specific trends, and recent incidents to prioritize threats.

Types of Threat Intelligence

- **Strategic Intelligence:**
  Provides high-level insights into threat trends and adversary motivations, useful for executive decision-making.

- **Operational Intelligence:**
  Focuses on the tactics and targets of adversaries, helping organizations prepare for imminent threats.

- **Tactical Intelligence:**
  Includes specific indicators (IP addresses, URLs, file hashes) that enable rapid detection and response.

- **Technical Intelligence:**
  Detailed data on vulnerabilities, exploits, and security tool performance to refine defensive measures.

Threat Intelligence Sharing and Collaboration

- **Information Sharing Communities:**
  Organizations often participate in industry-specific Information Sharing and Analysis Centers (ISACs) or similar groups to share intelligence.

- **Automated Sharing:**
  Integration with CTI platforms allows automated sharing of IOCs, enabling faster collective responses.

- **Collaboration:**
  Partnerships with government agencies and security vendors enhance the overall quality and reach of threat intelligence.

14.3 Implementing Cyber Threat Intelligence

Developing a robust CTI program involves integrating intelligence into your broader security strategy. Follow these steps to implement effective threat intelligence:

Step 1: Define Objectives and Scope

- **Set Clear Goals:**
  Determine what you want to achieve with CTI— whether it's early threat detection, improved incident response, or strategic planning.

- **Scope Determination:**
  Identify the assets, networks, and data that are most critical and determine which threat vectors need close monitoring.

- **Legal Considerations:**
  Ensure that your intelligence collection methods
  comply with legal and ethical standards.

Step 2: Establish a Data Collection Framework

- **Internal Data Sources:**
  Leverage SIEM logs, IDS/IPS alerts, and EDR data for
  insights on internal threats.

- **External Data Integration:**
  Subscribe to reputable threat feeds, monitor OSINT,
  and consider partnerships with CTI vendors.

- **Aggregation and Normalization:**
  Use tools or platforms that consolidate data into a
  standardized format for easier analysis.

Step 3: Analyze and Contextualize Threat Data

- **Deploy Analysis Tools:**
  Utilize platforms that offer advanced analytics, such as
  machine learning-based anomaly detection, to sift
  through large datasets.

- **Contextual Enrichment:**
  Enrich raw data with contextual information from
  external sources, providing a complete picture of threat
  activity.

- **Prioritize Threats:**
  Use risk assessment techniques to categorize threats
  based on potential impact and likelihood.

Step 4: Integrate CTI into Operational Processes

- **SIEM and SOAR Integration:**
  Feed CTI data into your SIEM for real-time correlation and into SOAR platforms to automate response actions.

- **Incident Response:**
  Ensure that CTI insights are a core part of your incident response plan, helping to swiftly identify and neutralize threats.

- **Decision-Making:**
  Use strategic intelligence to inform executive decisions on security investments and policy changes.

Step 5: Continuous Improvement and Collaboration

- **Feedback Loop:**
  Regularly review the effectiveness of your CTI program through post-incident analysis and ongoing audits.

- **Collaboration:**
  Share and receive intelligence from external partners and industry groups to keep your information current.

- **Training and Updates:**
  Keep your threat intelligence team updated on emerging trends and analytical methodologies.

Actionable Task

- **CTI Pilot Project:**
  Choose a specific business unit or critical asset to launch a CTI pilot project. Identify and aggregate data from internal and external sources, analyze it for patterns and IOCs, and integrate the intelligence into your SIEM system. Document the process, measure key

metrics (such as detection time improvements), and prepare a report summarizing your findings and recommended enhancements. Share this report with your security leadership team for further refinement.

- **Threat Intelligence Sharing Exercise:**
  Participate in an industry information-sharing group (or simulate one) by compiling and sharing a set of IOCs with peers. Evaluate the feedback and discuss how shared intelligence could improve your overall security posture.

14.4 Real-World Applications and Case Studies

Case Study 1: Enhancing Threat Detection in a Financial Institution

A mid-sized bank leveraged CTI to strengthen its security posture:

- **Data Aggregation:**
  The bank integrated internal logs from its SIEM with external threat feeds.

- **Analysis and Prioritization:**
  Analysts identified trends indicating a coordinated phishing campaign targeting financial transactions.

- **Operational Integration:**
  CTI data was fed into their SOAR platform, which automated several response tasks.

- **Outcome:**
  The bank improved its mean time to detect (MTTD) by

35% and reduced successful phishing incidents by 50%, significantly bolstering customer trust.

Case Study 2: Strategic Intelligence in a Global E-Commerce Company

A global e-commerce company utilized strategic CTI to inform its security investments:

- **Threat Landscape Analysis:**
  By analyzing adversary trends and global threat reports, the company identified emerging risks, including sophisticated malware targeting online transactions.

- **Informed Decision-Making:**
  The insights led to targeted investments in advanced endpoint protection and improved incident response protocols.

- **Outcome:**
  The company reported a 40% reduction in financial losses due to cyber-attacks and enhanced its ability to predict and counter emerging threats.

Global Insight:
A European technology firm integrated CTI with automated incident response, achieving a 50% improvement in proactive threat identification. Their approach, which combined external threat feeds with internal analytics, set a new standard for industry-wide collaboration and rapid defense.

14.5 Resources and Next Steps

To further enhance your CTI capabilities, consider the following resources:

- **Books:**

    o *"Cyber Threat Intelligence: How to Harness the Power of Information"*

    o *"The Threat Intelligence Handbook: A Practical Guide for Security Teams"*

- **Certifications:**

    o Consider certifications such as Certified Threat Intelligence Analyst (CTIA) or GIAC Cyber Threat Intelligence (GCTI) for advanced credentials.

- **Professional Organizations:**

    o Engage with the Cyber Threat Intelligence Integration Center (CTIIC), ISACA, and (ISC)^2 for networking, training, and industry insights.

- **Tools:**

    o Experiment with open-source threat intelligence platforms like MISP (Malware Information Sharing Platform) or integrate commercial feeds into your SIEM for hands-on practice.

- **Conferences and Workshops:**

    o Attend events such as the Cyber Threat Intelligence Summit or DEF CON CTI sessions to stay updated on the latest trends and techniques.

Practical Tip:
Start by setting up a CTI dashboard that aggregates data from key internal and external sources. Use this dashboard to monitor emerging threats and adjust your security strategies accordingly. Regularly review and update your threat models based on new intelligence.

14.6 Chapter Takeaways

Key Points:

- **Cyber Threat Intelligence (CTI)** transforms raw data into actionable insights about adversary tactics, enabling proactive defense.

- Core components of CTI include **data collection, threat analysis, contextualization, and collaborative sharing**.

- CTI provides different layers of intelligence—strategic, operational, tactical, and technical—that guide decision-making and incident response.

- Effective CTI implementation involves defining objectives, integrating internal and external data sources, and continuously monitoring for new threats.

- Real-world case studies demonstrate that robust CTI programs can significantly reduce detection times and enhance overall security posture.

- Continuous improvement, collaboration, and training are essential to maintain a dynamic and effective CTI capability.

14.7 Test Your Knowledge

1. **Which of the following best describes Cyber Threat Intelligence (CTI)?**
   A. A method to encrypt sensitive data
   B. The process of collecting and analyzing threat data to produce actionable insights
   C. A system for managing user access controls
   D. A tool for automating patch management

2. **What is one primary benefit of integrating external threat feeds into your CTI program?**
   A. It reduces the need for internal logging
   B. It enables proactive detection of emerging threats by incorporating global threat data
   C. It simplifies network architecture
   D. It eliminates the need for manual analysis

3. **Scenario Question:**
   Imagine you are the threat intelligence lead at a multinational organization. Describe one strategy you would use to enhance your CTI capabilities (for example, integrating a new threat feed or employing machine learning for anomaly detection), and explain how it would improve your organization's ability to anticipate and mitigate threats. Include specific tools or methodologies where applicable.

4. **Reflective Exercise:**
   Create a basic diagram that outlines your organization's CTI process, from data collection to analysis and dissemination. Identify one potential gap in your current CTI workflow and propose an improvement. Then, explain how you would test and communicate this improvement to your security team.

14.8 Final Thoughts

Cyber Threat Intelligence is a powerful tool that enables organizations to stay ahead of adversaries by converting vast amounts of data into actionable insights. By systematically collecting, analyzing, and contextualizing threat data, CTI provides the foresight necessary to anticipate attacks and bolster your cyber defenses. This chapter has offered a detailed exploration of CTI's core components, practical implementation steps, and real-world applications, supported by expert insights and actionable tasks.

As you continue through this book, the principles of CTI will complement other facets of cyber defense, such as risk management, network security, and incident response, to form a cohesive, proactive defense strategy. Embrace continuous learning and collaboration in your CTI efforts and remain agile in adapting to an ever-evolving threat landscape.

Thank you for exploring Chapter 14. Apply these insights and practical exercises to build a robust CTI program and continue your journey toward mastering cyber defense.

End of Chapter 14

Artificial Intelligence (AI) and Machine Learning (ML) have rapidly transformed the cybersecurity landscape. These technologies empower organizations to process massive volumes of data, detect subtle anomalies, and automate responses to emerging threats. In this chapter, we explore the role of AI and ML in enhancing cyber defenses. We'll examine key concepts, methodologies, and tools, and illustrate their application through real-world case studies. Building on the foundational principles discussed in earlier chapters, you will learn how to leverage AI and ML to predict, detect, and respond to cyber threats more effectively.

Expert Insight:
"AI and Machine Learning are not silver bullets, but they dramatically enhance our ability to detect complex threats by analyzing patterns and anomalies that traditional methods might miss." — Senior Cybersecurity Data Scientist

---

15.1 What Is AI and Machine Learning in Cybersecurity?

AI in cybersecurity refers to the use of advanced algorithms and computational models to simulate human intelligence for threat detection, analysis, and response. Machine Learning, a subset of AI, involves training models on historical data to identify patterns and make predictions. Together, these technologies enable:

- **Anomaly Detection:** Identifying unusual behavior that may indicate an attack.

- **Predictive Analysis:** Forecasting potential threats based on trends and historical incidents.

- **Automated Response:** Enabling rapid, automated reactions to detected threats.

- **Adaptive Security:** Continuously learning from new data to improve defenses over time.

By processing vast amounts of data faster than human analysts can, AI and ML help organizations detect subtle indicators of compromise and respond swiftly to mitigate damage.

15.2 Core Components and Techniques

A robust AI and ML strategy in cybersecurity comprises several critical components and techniques:

Data Collection and Preprocessing

- **Data Aggregation:**
  Collect data from various sources—SIEM logs, network traffic, endpoint monitoring, and threat intelligence feeds—to create a comprehensive dataset.

- **Data Cleansing:**
  Remove noise and irrelevant information to ensure that the machine learning models are trained on high-quality data.

- **Feature Engineering:**
  Identify and extract meaningful features that help distinguish normal behavior from anomalies.

Supervised Learning

- **Training Models:**
  Use labeled datasets, where historical incidents are marked as benign or malicious, to train classification models.

- **Common Algorithms:**
  Techniques like decision trees, support vector machines, and neural networks are widely used for threat detection.

- **Application:**
  For example, supervised learning can be used to classify network traffic as normal or suspicious based on prior attack data.

Unsupervised Learning

- **Anomaly Detection:**
  Apply clustering or outlier detection algorithms to identify unusual patterns that were not previously labeled.

- **Techniques:**
  Methods such as k-means clustering, DBSCAN, and autoencoders help in detecting previously unknown threats.

- **Advantage:**
  This approach is particularly useful for zero-day threats and novel attack vectors.

Reinforcement Learning

- **Adaptive Security:**
  Reinforcement learning models learn optimal

responses through trial and error, continuously improving their actions based on feedback from the environment.

- **Use Case:**
  Automated incident response systems can benefit from reinforcement learning by optimizing remediation steps over time.

Natural Language Processing (NLP)

- **Threat Intelligence Analysis:**
  NLP techniques can analyze textual data from sources like threat reports, forums, and news articles to extract indicators of compromise (IOCs) and emerging trends.

- **Integration:**
  This analysis enriches machine learning models by providing contextual insights from unstructured data.

15.3 Implementing AI and ML in Cybersecurity

Deploying AI and ML in a cybersecurity context requires a methodical approach that integrates these technologies into existing security operations.

Step 1: Define Objectives and Metrics

- **Set Clear Goals:**
  Determine whether the focus is on anomaly detection, predictive threat modeling, or automating incident response.

- **Establish Metrics:**
  Define key performance indicators (KPIs) such as

detection accuracy, false positive rates, Mean Time to Detect (MTTD), and Mean Time to Respond (MTTR).

Step 2: Data Collection and Model Training

- **Data Aggregation:**
  Collect and centralize data from multiple sources. Ensure that data is representative of the environment.

- **Model Selection:**
  Choose appropriate ML algorithms (supervised, unsupervised, reinforcement) based on your objectives.

- **Training and Validation:**
  Train models using historical data and validate them with test datasets to ensure accuracy and robustness.

Step 3: Integration into Security Operations

- **SIEM and SOAR Integration:**
  Feed AI-driven insights into your SIEM and SOAR platforms to enhance real-time detection and automate responses.

- **Alert Prioritization:**
  Use ML models to rank alerts based on risk, reducing alert fatigue for security teams.

- **Continuous Learning:**
  Implement feedback loops so that models can learn from new incidents, continuously improving their detection capabilities.

Step 4: Testing and Continuous Improvement

- **Simulated Attacks:**
  Conduct controlled simulations and red team exercises to test the effectiveness of AI/ML models.

- **Performance Monitoring:**
  Regularly review model performance metrics and adjust parameters as needed.

- **Incident Reviews:**
  Analyze incidents where AI/ML played a role in detection or response to refine models and processes.

Step 5: Training and Collaboration

- **Team Training:**
  Educate your security team on how to interpret AI/ML outputs and integrate them into decision-making processes.

- **Cross-Functional Collaboration:**
  Encourage collaboration between data scientists, security analysts, and IT staff to ensure models are aligned with operational realities.

Actionable Task

- **AI Pilot Project:**
  Choose a specific area, such as network traffic analysis, and implement an ML model for anomaly detection. Collect relevant data, train your model, and integrate it with your SIEM platform. Monitor its performance over a set period, document improvements in detection times, and prepare a report outlining the outcomes and next steps.

- **Model Evaluation Exercise:**
  Conduct a comparative analysis of at least two different ML algorithms (e.g., a decision tree vs. a neural network) for classifying potential threats in your environment. Evaluate their performance based on accuracy and false positive rates and document your findings in a brief report.

15.4 Real-World Applications and Case Studies

Case Study 1: Predictive Threat Detection in a Financial Institution

A mid-sized bank integrated AI-driven threat detection into its cybersecurity operations:

- **Data Aggregation:**
  The bank collected historical data from its SIEM, IDS/IPS, and endpoint logs.

- **Model Training:**
  Using supervised learning, a neural network was trained to distinguish between normal and malicious network behavior.

- **Operational Integration:**
  The model was integrated with the bank's SIEM, enabling real-time alert prioritization.

- **Outcome:**
  The bank experienced a 35% improvement in detection accuracy and a 30% reduction in the time taken to detect anomalies, significantly enhancing its overall security posture.

Case Study 2: Adaptive Incident Response in a Global E-Commerce Company

A global e-commerce company implemented reinforcement learning to optimize its automated incident response:

- **Adaptive Learning:**
  The company deployed a reinforcement learning model within its SOAR platform to automate containment procedures.

- **Real-Time Adjustments:**
  The model learned from previous incidents, refining its response strategies over time.

- **Integration with SIEM:**
  Combined with a SIEM system, the model could trigger automated containment actions upon detecting specific threat patterns.

- **Outcome:**
  The initiative reduced the Mean Time to Respond (MTTR) by 40% and provided a more adaptive, robust defense during peak transaction periods.

Global Insight:
A European technology firm used NLP to analyze threat intelligence reports, enriching their machine learning models with contextual insights. This integration led to a 50% reduction in false positives and significantly enhanced the firm's proactive threat detection capabilities.

15.5 Resources and Next Steps

To advance your knowledge and practical skills in AI and ML for cybersecurity, consider these resources:

- **Online Courses:**

  - Platforms such as Coursera, Udemy, and Cybrary offer specialized courses on machine learning, AI applications in cybersecurity, and data science for security.

- **Books:**

  - *"Machine Learning for Cybersecurity"*

  - *"Artificial Intelligence in Cybersecurity"*

- **Certifications:**

  - Consider certifications such as Certified Information Systems Security Professional (CISSP) with a focus on AI/ML, or specialized courses in cybersecurity data analytics.

- **Professional Organizations:**

  - Engage with organizations like (ISC)^2, ISACA, and the IEEE Cybersecurity Initiative for webinars, conferences, and networking opportunities.

- **Tools and Platforms:**

  - Experiment with open-source platforms like TensorFlow, Scikit-Learn, and open-source SIEM integrations to develop your own AI models for threat detection.

- **Conferences and Workshops:**
    - Attend events such as Black Hat, DEF CON, or AI-specific cybersecurity summits to stay updated on the latest trends and technologies.

Practical Tip:
Start by setting up a small-scale lab environment where you can safely experiment with AI models for anomaly detection. Use this lab to test different algorithms, analyze their performance, and iteratively improve your models before integrating them into your production environment.

15.6 Chapter Takeaways

Key Points:

- **AI and Machine Learning (ML) in Cybersecurity** leverage advanced algorithms to analyze vast datasets, detect anomalies, and automate threat responses.

- Core components include **data collection and preprocessing, supervised and unsupervised learning, reinforcement learning,** and **natural language processing (NLP)** for contextual threat intelligence.

- Implementing AI/ML requires a systematic approach: defining objectives, gathering quality data, training and validating models, and integrating these models into existing security systems like SIEM and SOAR.

- Real-world case studies demonstrate that AI-driven systems can significantly improve threat detection accuracy and response times.

- Continuous improvement through regular model updates, training, and cross-functional collaboration is essential to adapt to evolving cyber threats.

15.7 Test Your Knowledge

1. **Which of the following best describes the role of supervised learning in cybersecurity?**
   A. Identifying new threats without prior knowledge
   B. Training models on labeled datasets to classify network behavior
   C. Automating incident response actions
   D. Encrypting sensitive data

2. **What is one primary advantage of using unsupervised learning for threat detection?**
   A. It requires no data preprocessing
   B. It can identify unknown or zero-day threats by detecting anomalies
   C. It eliminates the need for human analysts
   D. It guarantees 100% detection accuracy

3. **Scenario Question:**
   Imagine you are the cybersecurity data scientist at a multinational organization. Describe one strategy you would use to integrate AI into your threat detection system and explain how you would measure its effectiveness. Include specific tools or methodologies that might be applied.

4. **Reflective Exercise:**
   Draw a simplified diagram of an AI-driven threat detection workflow, from data collection to automated response. Identify one potential challenge in

implementing this workflow, propose an improvement, and outline how you would communicate this to your security team.

15.8 Final Thoughts

AI and Machine Learning represent a paradigm shift in how organizations defend against cyber threats. By automating the detection of subtle anomalies, predicting potential attacks, and streamlining incident response, these technologies offer unprecedented capabilities in safeguarding digital assets. This chapter has provided a comprehensive overview of AI and ML applications in cybersecurity, covering core techniques, implementation strategies, and real-world examples that demonstrate tangible benefits.

As you progress in your journey to master cyber defense, remember that AI and ML are powerful tools that require continuous learning and adaptation. The insights you gain from deploying these technologies should be integrated with other aspects of your security strategy—such as risk management, network security, and incident response—to create a robust, layered defense. Embrace the challenge of staying ahead in an ever-evolving threat landscape by continually refining your models, leveraging emerging trends, and collaborating across disciplines.

Thank you for exploring Chapter 15. Apply these insights and practical exercises to enhance your AI-driven security capabilities, and continue your journey toward a smarter, more proactive cyber defense strategy.

End of Chapter 15

Quantum computing represents a paradigm shift in information
processing, harnessing the unique principles of quantum
mechanics to perform computations at unprecedented speeds.
However, these advances also pose a serious threat to many of
today's cryptographic systems. Post-Quantum Cryptography
(PQC) is the field dedicated to developing new cryptographic
algorithms that are resistant to quantum attacks. In this
chapter, we explore the fundamentals of quantum computing,
its impact on classical cryptography, and the emerging
solutions of PQC. Building on the core cyber defense concepts
discussed in earlier chapters, you will learn how to assess the
quantum threat, evaluate post-quantum algorithms, and plan
for a transition to quantum-resistant security.

Expert Insight:
"Quantum computing promises to revolutionize many
industries, but its potential to break current cryptographic
schemes makes post-quantum cryptography not just a future
consideration, but an immediate imperative for secure
systems." — Senior Cryptography Researcher

16.1 What Is Quantum Computing and Post-Quantum Cryptography?

Quantum computing uses quantum bits, or qubits, which can
exist in multiple states simultaneously—a property known as
superposition—and become interlinked through
entanglement. These principles enable quantum computers to

process vast amounts of data in parallel, dramatically accelerating complex computations.

While classical computers rely on bits that are either 0 or 1, qubits can represent both at once, allowing quantum algorithms such as Shor's algorithm and Grover's algorithm to solve problems, like factoring large numbers or searching unsorted databases, much faster than traditional methods. Shor's algorithm, in particular, poses a threat to widely used cryptographic systems such as RSA and ECC.

Post-Quantum Cryptography (PQC) seeks to develop cryptographic algorithms that can withstand quantum attacks. Unlike quantum cryptography, which leverages quantum principles for security, PQC focuses on classical algorithms that are inherently resistant to quantum computing capabilities. These new cryptographic techniques aim to protect data even in the presence of powerful quantum adversaries.

16.2 Core Components of Quantum Computing and Post-Quantum Cryptography

A comprehensive understanding of quantum computing and PQC involves several key components and concepts:

Quantum Computing Fundamentals

- **Qubits and Superposition:**
  Qubits are the building blocks of quantum computing. Unlike classical bits, qubits can represent multiple values simultaneously through superposition, enabling parallel computation.

- **Entanglement:**
When qubits become entangled, the state of one qubit instantly influences the state of another, no matter the distance between them. This property is fundamental to the potential power of quantum computers.

- **Quantum Algorithms:**
Algorithms like Shor's algorithm can factor large numbers exponentially faster than classical methods, while Grover's algorithm provides quadratic speedups in database search operations.

Threats to Classical Cryptography

- **Impact on RSA and ECC:**
Current cryptographic systems, such as RSA and Elliptic Curve Cryptography (ECC), rely on the difficulty of factoring large numbers and solving discrete logarithm problems—tasks that quantum computers could solve efficiently using Shor's algorithm.

- **Increased Vulnerability:**
As quantum computing matures, the window of vulnerability for existing cryptographic systems narrows, making the transition to quantum-resistant solutions critical.

Post-Quantum Cryptographic Techniques

- **Lattice-Based Cryptography:**
Based on the hardness of lattice problems, such as the Shortest Vector Problem (SVP), lattice-based algorithms are considered strong candidates for PQC.

- **Hash-Based Signatures:**
These rely on the security of cryptographic hash

functions. Although they typically produce larger signature sizes, they offer robust security guarantees.

- **Code-Based Cryptography:**
  Utilizing error-correcting codes, this approach has been well-studied and is known for its resilience against quantum attacks.

- **Multivariate Quadratic Equations:**
  This technique involves solving systems of quadratic equations over finite fields, a problem that is believed to be hard even for quantum computers.

- **Isogeny-Based Cryptography:**
  A newer area that leverages the properties of elliptic curves in a way that is resistant to quantum attacks, though it is still under active research.

16.3 Implementing Post-Quantum Cryptography

Transitioning to post-quantum cryptographic solutions requires careful planning and a phased approach:

Step 1: Risk Assessment and Inventory

- **Assess Vulnerable Systems:**
  Identify all cryptographic systems in use and assess their vulnerability to quantum attacks.

- **Data Sensitivity Analysis:**
  Prioritize systems and data based on sensitivity and the potential impact of a quantum breach.

Step 2: Research and Selection of PQC Algorithms

- **Evaluate Candidate Algorithms:**
  Review emerging PQC algorithms, such as those based on lattice-based and hash-based cryptography. Consider factors like computational efficiency, key sizes, and security assumptions.

- **Pilot Projects:**
  Conduct pilot projects to test the feasibility of integrating PQC algorithms into your existing systems. Use test environments to evaluate performance and compatibility.

Step 3: Develop an Integration Plan

- **Define Migration Strategies:**
  Create a roadmap for transitioning from classical cryptography to PQC. This may involve dual running both systems in parallel until PQC solutions are proven reliable.

- **Update Policies and Procedures:**
  Revise cryptographic policies to include PQC requirements. Ensure that compliance standards reflect the new technology.

- **Collaboration:**
  Work closely with cryptography experts and vendors to understand the practical challenges of implementing PQC.

Step 4: Implementation and Continuous Monitoring

- **Deploy PQC Solutions:**
  Roll out PQC algorithms in phases, starting with less

critical systems. Monitor performance and security metrics closely.

- **Integrate with Existing Systems:**
  Ensure that the new cryptographic methods are seamlessly integrated with current security frameworks, such as SIEM and IAM systems.

- **Regular Testing and Audits:**
  Perform ongoing assessments and stress tests to ensure that PQC implementations are robust and remain secure against emerging quantum threats.

Actionable Task

- **PQC Pilot Project:**
  Select a non-critical application or service that currently uses classical cryptography. Implement a pilot project by integrating a PQC algorithm (e.g., a lattice-based encryption scheme). Monitor its performance, evaluate key metrics such as encryption/decryption speed, and assess any impact on system resources. Document the process, compile findings, and prepare a report to inform your broader migration strategy.

- **Algorithm Comparison Exercise:**
  Evaluate at least two PQC algorithms using a controlled dataset. Compare their performance based on key size, computational overhead, and security assurances. Document your analysis and present recommendations for which algorithm(s) could be adopted organization wide.

16.4 Real-World Applications and Case Studies

Case Study 1: Financial Institution's Transition to PQC

A mid-sized bank, recognizing the impending threat of quantum computing, began its journey to adopt PQC:

- **Initial Assessment:**
  The bank conducted a comprehensive review of its cryptographic systems, identifying RSA-based encryption as a key vulnerability.

- **Pilot Implementation:**
  A lattice-based encryption algorithm was piloted in a non-critical segment of the banking application. The pilot demonstrated acceptable performance metrics and strong resistance to simulated quantum attacks.

- **Outcome:**
  The pilot project paved the way for a phased migration plan, reducing the bank's long-term risk profile and positioning it to meet future regulatory requirements.

Case Study 2: Government Agency Adopts PQC for Secure Communications

A government agency responsible for sensitive communications faced growing concerns over the quantum threat:

- **Threat Landscape Analysis:**
  The agency analyzed the potential impact of quantum computing on its encrypted communications.

- **Dual Cryptography Approach:**
  The agency deployed a dual cryptography model, running classical and post-quantum algorithms in

parallel. This allowed for a gradual transition without disrupting operational integrity.

- **Outcome:**
  The agency reported enhanced security and readiness for the quantum era, with periodic audits confirming the robustness of the PQC systems and minimal impact on communication efficiency.

Global Insight:

A European technology consortium integrated PQC into its research and development processes, achieving a 50% improvement in resistance to simulated quantum attacks. Their collaborative approach, which included industry, academia, and government partners, has set a benchmark for PQC adoption across sectors.

16.5 Resources and Next Steps

To further advance your knowledge and implementation of post-quantum cryptography, consider the following resources:

- **Online Courses:**

  - Coursera, Udemy, and Cybrary offer courses on quantum computing fundamentals, PQC algorithms, and cryptographic engineering.

- **Books:**

  - *"Quantum Computing for Computer Scientists"*

  - *"Post-Quantum Cryptography"* by Daniel J. Bernstein, Johannes Buchmann, and Erik Dahmen.

- **Certifications:**

  - Explore emerging certifications and specialized training in quantum-safe cryptography.

- **Professional Organizations:**

  - Engage with organizations like the International Association for Cryptologic Research (IACR) and the National Institute of Standards and Technology (NIST) for updates on PQC standards and research.

- **Tools and Platforms:**

  - Experiment with open-source PQC libraries and simulation tools, such as the NIST PQC candidate algorithms available for testing.

- **Conferences and Workshops:**

  - Attend events focused on quantum computing and cryptography, such as the PQCrypto conference or workshops hosted by the Cloud Security Alliance (CSA).

Practical Tip:
Start by conducting a vulnerability assessment of your current cryptographic systems, focusing on those that may be susceptible to quantum attacks. Use this assessment to identify priority areas for a pilot PQC project and establish a timeline for gradual migration.

16.6 Chapter Takeaways

Key Points:

- **Quantum Computing** leverages quantum mechanics to perform complex computations at unprecedented speeds, posing a significant threat to current cryptographic methods.

- **Post-Quantum Cryptography (PQC)** is focused on developing new cryptographic algorithms that are resistant to quantum attacks, ensuring the long-term security of digital communications.

- Core components include understanding quantum principles (superposition, entanglement), evaluating the impact of quantum algorithms (like Shor's and Grover's), and implementing PQC techniques such as lattice-based, hash-based, code-based, and multivariate cryptography.

- A systematic approach to implementing PQC involves assessing current vulnerabilities, selecting and piloting PQC algorithms, integrating them into existing systems, and continuously monitoring their performance.

- Real-world case studies demonstrate that early adoption of PQC can reduce long-term risk and ensure compliance with emerging standards in a quantum-threat landscape.

- Continuous research, collaboration, and adaptation are essential to maintain a robust cryptographic posture in the face of advancing quantum technology.

16.7 Test Your Knowledge

1. **Which of the following best describes the concept of superposition in quantum computing?**
   A. The ability of a qubit to exist in multiple states simultaneously
   B. The process of entangling two qubits
   C. A method to encrypt data using quantum keys
   D. The speed at which classical computers process information

2. **What is the primary goal of Post-Quantum Cryptography (PQC)?**
   A. To enhance classical encryption algorithms with additional keys
   B. To develop cryptographic systems that are secure against quantum computing attacks
   C. To create quantum computers for faster processing
   D. To replace all digital communication with quantum channels

3. **Scenario Question:**
   Imagine you are a security architect for a multinational corporation. You have been tasked with evaluating the risks posed by quantum computing to your current cryptographic systems. Describe one specific PQC algorithm you would consider (e.g., a lattice-based scheme), and explain how you would implement a pilot project to test its performance and security. Include how you would measure the success of this pilot.

4. **Reflective Exercise:**
   Create a simplified diagram outlining the transition from classical cryptography to post-quantum cryptography in your organization. Identify two critical

systems that rely on vulnerable cryptographic methods, propose a mitigation strategy using PQC techniques, and outline how you would communicate this transition plan to both technical and non-technical stakeholders.

16.8 Final Thoughts

Quantum computing poses a transformative challenge to modern cryptography, but it also drives innovation in creating quantum-resistant solutions. By understanding the fundamental principles of quantum computing and implementing robust post-quantum cryptography, organizations can future-proof their security frameworks against emerging threats. This chapter has provided a detailed overview of the key concepts, implementation strategies, and real-world applications of PQC, supported by actionable tasks and expert insights.

As you continue your journey through this book, remember that staying ahead in cybersecurity requires continuous adaptation and proactive planning. The principles discussed here, combined with those from previous chapters, form a comprehensive defense strategy that addresses both current and future challenges.

Thank you for exploring Chapter 16. Apply these insights and practical exercises to begin your transition to quantum-resistant security and continue your journey toward mastering cyber defense in an evolving technological landscape.

End of Chapter 16

The proliferation of Internet of Things (IoT) devices and Operational Technology (OT) systems has transformed modern business and industrial environments. However, the rapid integration of these connected systems brings unique security challenges. In this chapter, we explore the principles and practices of securing IoT and OT environments. We discuss the fundamental differences between IT, IoT, and OT, the core components required for protecting these systems, and actionable strategies to safeguard them against emerging threats. Drawing on real-world case studies and expert insights, you'll learn how to build a resilient defense that spans both consumer-grade IoT devices and critical industrial control systems.

Expert Insight:
"Securing IoT and OT is not simply about applying traditional IT security measures—it requires understanding the unique operational constraints and threat landscapes of these environments. A tailored approach that addresses both connectivity and physical processes is essential." — Senior OT Security Specialist

---

17.1 What Is IoT and OT Security?

IoT security focuses on protecting a network of interconnected devices—ranging from smart appliances and wearables to industrial sensors and cameras—from unauthorized access and exploitation. OT security, on the other hand, involves safeguarding systems that control physical processes in industries like manufacturing, energy, transportation, and utilities. These systems, which include Supervisory Control and Data Acquisition (SCADA) systems and Distributed Control Systems (DCS), are critical for maintaining operational integrity and public safety.

Key objectives of IoT and OT security include:

- **Confidentiality:** Ensuring that sensitive operational data remains accessible only to authorized users.

- **Integrity:** Protecting data and system commands from tampering, which could lead to dangerous malfunctions.

- **Availability:** Guaranteeing that essential systems remain functional, even in the face of cyber-attacks or operational disruptions.

Due to the distinct nature of IoT and OT—often characterized by legacy systems, real-time operational demands, and physical safety implications—the security strategies must be customized accordingly.

17.2 Core Components of IoT and OT Security

A comprehensive security program for IoT and OT environments is built on multiple layers, combining both traditional IT measures and specialized controls. Key components include:

Device Security and Hardening

- **Firmware Integrity:** Ensure that device firmware is regularly updated and digitally signed to prevent tampering.

- **Physical Security:** Protect devices from physical access that could allow direct manipulation or theft.

- **Configuration Management:** Implement secure default settings and restrict unnecessary services on devices.

Network Segmentation and Isolation

- **Segmentation:** Divide networks into isolated segments to prevent lateral movement of attackers. For example, separate IoT devices from critical OT networks.

- **Firewalls and Access Controls:** Deploy specialized firewalls and network access controls to manage traffic between different network zones.

- **Zero Trust Principles:** Even within segmented networks, apply strict verification for every connection to minimize the risk of internal threats.

Secure Communication

- **Encryption:** Encrypt data in transit to protect communication between IoT devices and central systems. Protocols such as TLS/SSL are vital.

- **VPNs and Secure Tunnels:** For remote access, use VPNs to create secure, encrypted channels.

- **Authentication Protocols:** Implement robust authentication mechanisms to verify device identities before granting access.

Monitoring and Anomaly Detection

- **Real-Time Monitoring:** Use specialized monitoring systems that continuously track network traffic, device behavior, and system logs.

- **Anomaly Detection:** Deploy machine learning and behavioral analytics to detect deviations from normal operational patterns.

- **Integration with SIEM:** Feed IoT and OT logs into a centralized SIEM platform for comprehensive threat correlation and faster incident response.

Patch Management and Vulnerability Management

- **Regular Updates:** Establish procedures for timely patching of vulnerabilities in both IoT and OT systems, despite challenges posed by legacy hardware.

- **Vulnerability Scanning:** Regularly scan devices and networks to identify potential security gaps.

- **Risk-Based Prioritization:** Prioritize patching efforts based on the criticality of devices and the potential impact of vulnerabilities.

Specialized OT Security Controls

- **SCADA and ICS Security:** Implement controls specifically designed for Supervisory Control and Data Acquisition (SCADA) systems and industrial control systems.

- **Physical Process Protection:** Integrate cybersecurity with physical safety measures to ensure that attacks cannot cause real-world harm.

- **Vendor and Third-Party Management:** Ensure that all third-party devices and systems meet stringent security standards before integration.

17.3 Implementing IoT and OT Security

Deploying a robust security strategy for IoT and OT environments requires a structured approach that addresses both technical and operational challenges.

Step 1: Asset Inventory and Risk Assessment

- **Comprehensive Inventory:**
  Catalog all IoT and OT devices, including their firmware versions, network connections, and physical locations.

- **Risk Evaluation:**
  Assess the vulnerabilities of each device and the potential impact on operations. Use a risk matrix to prioritize which assets require immediate attention.

Step 2: Policy Development and Governance

- **Security Policies:**
  Develop policies that define the acceptable use, update procedures, and incident response protocols for IoT and OT devices.

- **Compliance and Standards:**
  Ensure that policies comply with relevant industry standards and regulations, such as NIST guidelines for OT and IoT.

- **Vendor Management:**
  Establish criteria for selecting and maintaining relationships with vendors to ensure that devices meet your security requirements.

Step 3: Deploy and Harden Security Controls

- **Device Hardening:**
  Configure devices securely by disabling unnecessary services, enforcing strong authentication, and regularly updating firmware.

- **Network Controls:**
  Segment networks and implement strict access controls using firewalls, VPNs, and Zero Trust principles.

- **Secure Communication:**
  Encrypt data in transit and deploy secure tunneling protocols to protect communications between devices and control centers.

- **Monitoring Tools:**
  Implement real-time monitoring systems and anomaly detection tools that integrate with your SIEM platform for continuous oversight.

Step 4: Continuous Monitoring and Response

- **Real-Time Analysis:**
  Use monitoring tools to continuously assess device behavior and network traffic, detecting anomalies early.

- **Automated Alerts:**
  Configure automated alerts for suspicious activities, such as unexpected communication patterns or failed authentication attempts.

- **Incident Response:**
  Develop and regularly test incident response plans that include specific protocols for IoT and OT environments.

Step 5: Training and Awareness

- **Specialized Training:**
  Provide targeted training for staff managing IoT and OT systems, emphasizing the unique security challenges of these environments.

- **Cross-Functional Workshops:**
  Conduct workshops that bring together IT, OT, and security teams to foster collaboration and share best practices.

- **User Awareness:**
  Educate all users on the importance of securing connected devices, including safe practices for remote work and device management.

Actionable Task

- **IoT/OT Security Assessment:**
  Conduct an inventory of all IoT and OT devices within your organization. Create a risk assessment matrix categorizing devices by their criticality and vulnerability. Identify one high-risk device and draft a remediation plan that includes firmware updates, network segmentation, and enhanced access controls.

- **Policy Drafting Exercise:**
  Draft a sample security policy for IoT and OT environments. Include guidelines for secure configuration, patch management, and incident response specific to these devices. Share the draft with both technical and operational teams for feedback and refinement.

17.4 Real-World Applications and Case Studies

Case Study 1: Securing Industrial Control Systems in a Manufacturing Plant

A large manufacturing plant faced challenges securing its operational technology:

- **Asset Inventory:**
  The plant conducted a comprehensive inventory of its OT devices, including SCADA systems and PLCs (Programmable Logic Controllers).

- **Network Segmentation:**
  The OT network was segmented from the corporate IT network, reducing the risk of lateral movement.

- **Continuous Monitoring:**
  Specialized monitoring tools were deployed to detect anomalies in control systems, integrating data with the central SIEM.

- **Outcome:**
  The plant experienced a 50% reduction in incidents related to unauthorized access and improved operational continuity even during targeted attacks.

Case Study 2: Enhancing IoT Security in a Global Smart City Initiative

A global smart city project, involving interconnected sensors, cameras, and environmental monitors, implemented a robust IoT security strategy:

- **Device Hardening:**
  All IoT devices were configured with secure firmware and regularly updated to address vulnerabilities.

- **Encryption and Secure Communication:**
  Data transmitted between devices and the central management system was encrypted using TLS.

- **Risk Management:**
  A risk-based approach prioritized the protection of devices critical to public safety, such as traffic management sensors.

- **Outcome:**
  The initiative achieved a 60% reduction in successful cyber intrusions and set new standards for smart city security protocols, ensuring both citizen safety and data integrity.

Global Insight:
A European energy company secured its OT and IoT assets by integrating specialized monitoring and anomaly detection systems, achieving a 55% improvement in early threat detection and significantly reducing downtime during security incidents.

17.5 Resources and Next Steps

To expand your knowledge and enhance your IoT and OT security practices, consider these resources:

- **Online Courses:**
  - Platforms like Coursera, Udemy, and Cybrary offer courses on IoT security, OT cybersecurity, and industrial control system protection.

- **Books:**

- o *"IoT Security: Advances in Authentication"*

- o *"Operational Technology Cybersecurity"* for industry-specific insights.

- **Certifications:**

  - o Consider certifications such as Global Industrial Cyber Security Professional (GICSP) or Certified IoT Security Practitioner (CIoTSP).

- **Professional Organizations:**

  - o Engage with the Industrial Internet Consortium (IIC), ISA/IEC, and the Cloud Security Alliance (CSA) for training, webinars, and networking opportunities.

- **Tools and Platforms:**

  - o Experiment with open-source IoT security frameworks, vulnerability scanners, and network segmentation tools to gain hands-on experience.

- **Conferences and Workshops:**

  - o Attend events such as the IoT World Conference or ISC West to stay current on emerging trends and best practices.

Practical Tip:
Begin by performing a detailed inventory and risk assessment of your IoT and OT assets. Use the insights to segment your networks and prioritize high-risk devices for immediate remediation. Establish a regular review schedule to keep your security measures updated.

17.6 Chapter Takeaways

Key Points:

- **IoT and OT Security** is vital for protecting the myriads of connected devices and industrial control systems that drive modern business and public infrastructure.

- Core components include **device hardening, network segmentation, secure communication, continuous monitoring,** and **specialized OT controls**.

- Effective security strategies require a systematic approach: asset inventory and risk assessment, policy development, deployment of technical controls, continuous monitoring, and ongoing training.

- Real-world case studies illustrate significant improvements in security posture—such as a 50–60% reduction in security incidents—when tailored IoT and OT security measures are implemented.

- Continuous adaptation to emerging threats and integration of best practices is essential to protect these unique environments.

17.7 Test Your Knowledge

1. **Which of the following best describes the primary objective of network segmentation in IoT and OT security?**
   A. To increase network speed
   B. To restrict lateral movement of attackers and isolate critical systems

C. To simplify device configuration

D. To automate firmware updates

2. **What is one key function of secure communication in IoT environments?**

A. To enhance device performance

B. To ensure that data transmitted between devices is encrypted and protected from interception

C. To provide remote access without authentication

D. To monitor physical device locations

3. **Scenario Question:**

Imagine you are the security manager for a smart city project. Describe one strategy you would implement to secure IoT devices used in traffic management and explain how you would measure its effectiveness. Include specific tools or methodologies that might be applied.

4. **Reflective Exercise:**

Draw a simplified diagram of an OT network within an industrial setting, identifying key assets and potential vulnerabilities. For each identified risk, propose one mitigation strategy and outline how you would update your security policies to incorporate these improvements. Explain how you would communicate these changes to both technical staff and non-technical management.

17.8 Final Thoughts

Securing IoT and OT environments is a complex but critical aspect of modern cyber defense. The unique challenges presented by interconnected devices and industrial control systems require tailored security measures that address both digital and physical risks. This chapter has provided a comprehensive overview of the key components, implementation strategies, and real-world applications necessary for effective IoT and OT security. By integrating robust device hardening, network segmentation, secure communication, and continuous monitoring into your defense strategy, you can protect critical assets and ensure operational continuity.

As you move forward in this book, the principles discussed here will integrate with other core areas—such as risk management, network security, and endpoint security—to form a cohesive and resilient cyber defense framework. Continuous review, training, and adaptation to emerging threats are essential to maintaining security in an ever-evolving landscape.

Thank you for exploring Chapter 17. Apply these insights and actionable tasks to strengthen your IoT and OT security posture and continue your journey toward mastering cyber defense.

End of Chapter 17

Critical infrastructure—such as power grids, water treatment facilities, transportation systems, and communication networks—forms the backbone of modern society. Protecting these vital systems from cyber threats is essential not only for business continuity but also for national security and public safety. In this chapter, we explore the unique challenges and strategies for securing critical infrastructure. We will delve into key concepts, core components, and implementation practices tailored to these complex environments. Drawing on real-world case studies and actionable tasks, you will learn how to build a resilient cybersecurity framework that addresses both the digital and physical dimensions of critical infrastructure.

Expert Insight:
"Securing critical infrastructure is about ensuring that essential services remain uninterrupted in the face of evolving cyber threats. It requires a multi-layered approach that integrates technical, operational, and strategic defenses." — National Security Advisor

18.1 What Is Cybersecurity in Critical Infrastructure?

Cybersecurity in critical infrastructure focuses on protecting systems that provide essential services to society. These systems often blend traditional IT components with operational technology (OT) that controls physical processes. The primary objectives include:

- **Confidentiality:** Preventing unauthorized access to sensitive operational data.

- **Integrity:** Ensuring that control systems function as intended without malicious tampering.

- **Availability:** Guaranteeing continuous operation, even during cyber-attacks or technical failures.

Given the potential for catastrophic consequences—ranging from power outages to compromised public safety—critical infrastructure requires tailored security measures that address both cyber and physical vulnerabilities.

18.2 Core Components of Cybersecurity in Critical Infrastructure

Effective protection of critical infrastructure relies on a combination of advanced technologies, robust processes, and coordinated response strategies. The key components include:

Risk Management and Asset Inventory

- **Asset Inventory:**
  Conduct a comprehensive inventory of all assets, including control systems, sensors, and network components.

- **Risk Assessment:**
  Identify vulnerabilities and potential threats specific to each asset. Use risk matrices and metrics like Annualized Loss Expectancy (ALE) to prioritize risks.

- **Operational Impact Analysis:**
  Assess the potential impact on public safety, business continuity, and national security.

Network and OT Segmentation

- **Network Segmentation:**
  Divide the infrastructure into isolated segments to prevent lateral movement of attackers.

- **OT Isolation:**
  Segregate operational technology networks from corporate IT systems, employing dedicated communication channels and strict access controls.

- **Zero Trust Principles:**
  Apply continuous verification even within segmented networks to ensure only authorized interactions occur.

Advanced Monitoring and Detection

- **SIEM Integration:**
  Aggregate logs from IT and OT systems into a centralized SIEM for real-time analysis.

- **Anomaly Detection:**
  Leverage machine learning and behavioral analytics to identify deviations from normal operations in both digital and physical control systems.

- **SCADA and ICS Monitoring:**
  Deploy specialized monitoring tools designed for Supervisory Control and Data Acquisition (SCADA) systems and Industrial Control Systems (ICS).

Incident Response and Recovery

- **Incident Response Planning:**
  Develop tailored incident response plans that address both IT and OT environments. Include procedures for containment, eradication, and system recovery.

- **Disaster Recovery and Business Continuity:**
  Establish robust backup and recovery processes, ensuring that critical services can be restored swiftly after an incident.

- **Cross-Functional Coordination:**
  Integrate response efforts between cybersecurity teams and operational staff to address both digital and physical impacts.

Physical Security and Access Control

- **Physical Barriers:**
  Implement physical security measures (e.g., access controls, surveillance) to protect critical facilities and hardware.

- **Environmental Controls:**
  Monitor physical parameters (temperature, humidity, vibrations) that could indicate tampering or failure.

- **Vendor and Supply Chain Security:**
  Ensure that third-party equipment and software meet rigorous security standards before integration.

Compliance and Regulatory Alignment

- **Regulatory Requirements:**
  Align security practices with industry-specific regulations (e.g., NERC CIP for energy, TSA guidelines for transportation).

- **Audit and Reporting:**
  Regularly conduct audits to verify compliance and generate detailed reports for regulators and stakeholders.

- **Policy Development:**
  Establish clear policies that address both cyber and physical aspects of critical infrastructure protection.

18.3 Implementing Cybersecurity in Critical Infrastructure

Implementing robust security for critical infrastructure requires a strategic, multi-phase approach that integrates technology, processes, and personnel. Follow these steps to build a resilient defense:

Step 1: Asset Inventory and Risk Assessment

- **Comprehensive Inventory:**
  Document all IT and OT assets, including hardware, control systems, and network devices.

- **Risk Evaluation:**
  Use qualitative and quantitative methods to assess vulnerabilities and prioritize risks. Consider both the potential cyber impact and the physical consequences.

- **Impact Analysis:**
  Evaluate how a security breach could affect service continuity and public safety.

Step 2: Develop and Enforce Security Policies

- **Policy Creation:**
  Develop security policies specific to critical infrastructure, addressing both cyber and physical risks. For example, establish strict access controls and update procedures for OT systems.

- **Compliance Alignment:**
  Ensure that policies meet industry standards and regulatory requirements (e.g., NERC CIP, ISO 27001).

- **Communication:**
  Clearly disseminate these policies through training sessions, manuals, and regular briefings.

Step 3: Deploy Segmentation and Monitoring Tools

- **Network Segmentation:**
  Implement VLANs, firewalls, and isolation techniques to divide IT and OT environments.

- **Advanced Monitoring:**
  Deploy SIEM systems and specialized OT monitoring tools to collect and analyze data in real-time.

- **Anomaly Detection:**
  Integrate machine learning-based tools to detect unusual patterns in operational data, ensuring early warning of potential threats.

Step 4: Establish Incident Response and Recovery Procedures

- **Incident Response Plan:**
  Develop a comprehensive response plan that includes containment, eradication, and recovery for both cyber and physical incidents.

- **Cross-Functional Teams:**
  Assemble teams that include IT security, OT engineers, and physical security personnel to ensure a coordinated response.

- **Drills and Simulations:**
  Regularly test response plans with simulations and tabletop exercises to identify gaps and refine procedures.

Step 5: Continuous Training and Policy Review

- **Employee Training:**
  Provide ongoing training for both IT and OT staff on security best practices, threat awareness, and incident response protocols.

- **Regular Audits:**
  Schedule periodic reviews of security policies, system configurations, and risk assessments.

- **Feedback Loop:**
  Incorporate lessons learned from drills and actual incidents to continuously improve security measures.

Actionable Task

- **Critical Infrastructure Security Assessment:**
  Perform a comprehensive inventory of your critical infrastructure assets. Create a risk assessment matrix that categorizes assets by their criticality and vulnerability. Choose one high-risk asset and develop a remediation plan that includes network segmentation, enhanced monitoring, and updated access controls. Document your process and review it with relevant stakeholders.

- **Policy Drafting Exercise:**
  Draft a security policy tailored to your critical infrastructure. Ensure the policy covers both cyber and physical security aspects, such as strict access controls,

regular patching schedules, and emergency response procedures. Share this draft with your cross-functional team for review and refinement.

18.4 Real-World Applications and Case Studies

Case Study 1: Securing a National Power Grid

A national power grid operator faced significant cybersecurity challenges due to legacy systems and extensive interconnectivity:

- **Asset Inventory and Segmentation:**
  The operator conducted a thorough asset inventory and segmented its network into isolated zones, separating critical control systems from administrative networks.

- **Advanced Monitoring:**
  SIEM systems and specialized SCADA monitoring tools were deployed to continuously monitor network traffic and operational data.

- **Incident Response:**
  A comprehensive incident response plan was implemented, reducing downtime during simulated attacks by 40%.

- **Outcome:**
  The power grid operator significantly enhanced its resilience, reducing the risk of cascading failures and improving overall reliability.

Case Study 2: Enhancing Security in Transportation Infrastructure

A major metropolitan transportation authority sought to protect its integrated network of signaling systems, ticketing machines, and operational controls:

- **Risk Assessment and Compliance:**
  A detailed risk assessment identified vulnerabilities in outdated signaling systems and unpatched software.

- **Policy and Controls:**
  The authority implemented strict access controls, encrypted data transmissions, and isolated critical systems using network segmentation.

- **Monitoring and Incident Response:**
  Real-time monitoring and a well-practiced incident response plan led to rapid detection and mitigation of a targeted cyber-attack.

- **Outcome:**
  The authority achieved a 50% reduction in security incidents, ensuring uninterrupted service and bolstering public confidence in its transportation network.

Global Insight:
A European water treatment facility integrated cybersecurity with physical security measures by using advanced monitoring tools and stringent access controls, achieving a 55% improvement in early threat detection and ensuring both operational continuity and public safety.

18.5 Resources and Next Steps

To further strengthen your knowledge and implementation of cybersecurity in critical infrastructure, consider these resources:

- **Online Courses:**

  - Coursera, Udemy, and Cybrary offer courses on critical infrastructure protection, industrial control system security, and SCADA security.

- **Books:**

  - *"Industrial Network Security"* by Eric D. Knapp

  - *"Cybersecurity for Critical Infrastructure Protection"*

- **Certifications:**

  - Look into certifications such as Global Industrial Cyber Security Professional (GICSP) or Certified SCADA Security Architect (CSSA).

- **Professional Organizations:**

  - Engage with organizations like the Industrial Internet Consortium (IIC), ISA, and the Cloud Security Alliance (CSA) for the latest insights and networking opportunities.

- **Tools:**

  - Experiment with open-source vulnerability scanners, network segmentation tools, and SCADA security platforms.

- **Conferences and Workshops:**

  - Attend industry events such as the Critical Infrastructure Protection Conference or ISC West to stay informed about emerging trends and best practices.

Practical Tip:
Begin by performing a detailed risk assessment of your critical infrastructure. Focus on segmenting networks, enhancing monitoring systems, and developing a clear incident response plan that integrates both cyber and physical security measures. Document your findings and set up a regular review schedule.

18.6 Chapter Takeaways

Key Points:

- **Cybersecurity in Critical Infrastructure** focuses on protecting systems that provide essential services, balancing both cyber and physical security.

- Core components include **risk management, network segmentation, advanced monitoring, incident response,** and **physical security controls**.

- A systematic approach involves detailed asset inventory, policy development, deployment of tailored security technologies, and continuous monitoring.

- Real-world case studies demonstrate that robust security measures can reduce incident rates by 50–60%, ensuring service continuity and public safety.

- Continuous improvement, regular training, and cross-functional coordination are essential to protect critical infrastructure against evolving threats.

18.7 Test Your Knowledge

1. **Which of the following best describes the purpose of network segmentation in critical infrastructure security?**
   A. To improve network speed
   B. To restrict lateral movement of attackers and isolate critical systems
   C. To simplify system configuration
   D. To automate patch management

2. **What is one key function of secure communication in critical infrastructure environments?**
   A. To allow unrestricted access to operational data
   B. To ensure that data transmitted between systems is encrypted and protected
   C. To reduce the cost of network hardware
   D. To monitor physical asset locations

3. **Scenario Question:**
   Imagine you are the cybersecurity manager for a national transportation authority. Describe one strategy you would implement to secure your critical signaling systems and explain how you would measure its effectiveness. Include specific tools or methodologies in your answer.

4. **Reflective Exercise:**
   Draw a simplified diagram of a critical infrastructure network (e.g., a power grid or water treatment facility).

Identify key assets and potential vulnerabilities, then propose one security improvement for each segment. Finally, outline how you would update your security policies and communicate these changes to both technical staff and non-technical management.

18.8 Final Thoughts

Securing critical infrastructure is a multifaceted challenge that demands a comprehensive, layered approach. By integrating robust cyber defenses with physical security measures, organizations can protect essential services against both digital and physical threats. This chapter has provided an in-depth exploration of the strategies, technologies, and best practices essential for safeguarding critical infrastructure—from detailed risk assessments and network segmentation to advanced monitoring and incident response. Real-world case studies underscore the tangible benefits of these measures, demonstrating significant reductions in security incidents and improved operational resilience.

As you progress through this book, the concepts and strategies discussed here will integrate with other core areas—such as risk management, network security, and endpoint security—to form a cohesive, resilient defense framework. Continuous adaptation, regular training, and proactive planning are key to maintaining security in an ever-evolving threat landscape.

Thank you for exploring Chapter 18. Apply these insights and actionable tasks to fortify your critical infrastructure, ensuring that your essential services remain secure and operational in the face of emerging threats.

End of Chapter 18

Part 4: Governance, Compliance, and Strategy

Chapter 19: Cybersecurity Governance

Cybersecurity Governance establishes the strategic framework, policies, and oversight necessary to align security initiatives with business objectives. It defines the roles and responsibilities of senior leadership, ensures accountability across the organization, and guides the implementation of technical and operational controls. In this chapter, we explore the key components of cybersecurity governance, discuss best practices for establishing effective oversight, and examine how to integrate governance into overall cyber defense strategy. Building on the risk management, network security, and compliance concepts from earlier chapters, you will learn how to create a robust governance framework that drives security as a business priority.

Expert Insight:
"Cybersecurity governance is not just an IT issue—it's a board-level imperative. Effective governance ensures that security investments and policies align with business goals while managing risk and ensuring compliance." — Chief Information Security Officer

19.1 What Is Cybersecurity Governance?

Cybersecurity governance encompasses the processes, policies, and structures that enable an organization to manage its cyber risks and secure its digital assets. It involves defining roles and responsibilities at the executive and operational levels, establishing clear policies, and ensuring that all security efforts support the organization's strategic objectives. Key objectives include:

- **Alignment:** Ensuring that cybersecurity strategies align with business goals and risk appetite.

- **Accountability:** Defining roles and responsibilities so that senior management and board members are actively involved in security oversight.

- **Compliance:** Establishing policies that meet regulatory requirements and industry standards.

- **Continuous Improvement:** Fostering an environment of ongoing assessment and enhancement of security practices.

Effective governance creates a culture where cybersecurity is integrated into all aspects of the organization, from strategic planning to daily operations.

19.2 Core Components of Cybersecurity Governance

A robust governance framework incorporates several critical components that work together to manage risk and drive continuous improvement:

Board and Executive Involvement

- **Leadership Engagement:**
  Involve senior executives and board members in cybersecurity discussions to ensure alignment with business strategy.

- **Strategic Oversight:**
  Develop committees or designate officers (e.g., Chief Information Security Officer) responsible for cybersecurity governance.

- **Reporting:**
  Implement regular reporting structures to keep leadership informed of security posture, incident trends, and compliance issues.

Policy Development and Documentation

- **Comprehensive Policies:**
  Create and maintain detailed policies covering data protection, incident response, access management, and more.

- **Standard Operating Procedures (SOPs):**
  Develop SOPs that outline how policies are implemented and enforced across the organization.

- **Regular Reviews:**
  Schedule periodic reviews and updates to policies to ensure they remain relevant in the face of evolving threats and regulatory changes.

Risk Management Integration

- **Risk Assessment:**
  Incorporate risk management into governance by ensuring that cybersecurity policies address identified risks.

- **Metrics and KPIs:**
  Establish key performance indicators (KPIs) such as

Mean Time to Detect (MTTD) and Mean Time to Respond (MTTR) to evaluate effectiveness.

- **Continuous Improvement:**
  Use post-incident reviews and audits to refine risk management practices and update policies accordingly.

Compliance and Regulatory Alignment

- **Adherence to Standards:**
  Ensure that governance frameworks align with regulatory requirements (e.g., GDPR, HIPAA, NERC CIP) and industry standards (e.g., ISO 27001, NIST CSF).

- **Audit and Reporting:**
  Regularly conduct internal and external audits and generate compliance reports to validate adherence.

- **Legal Oversight:**
  Involve legal teams to navigate complex regulatory landscapes and mitigate potential liabilities.

Communication and Training

- **Stakeholder Engagement:**
  Communicate cybersecurity policies and risk assessments across the organization to foster a culture of security.

- **Training Programs:**
  Provide regular training to ensure that employees understand their roles in maintaining security and complying with policies.

- **Feedback Mechanisms:**
  Create channels for staff to report concerns and suggest

improvements, ensuring continuous dialogue between leadership and operational teams.

19.3 Implementing Cybersecurity Governance

Building an effective cybersecurity governance framework requires a structured approach that integrates strategic planning, risk management, and continuous monitoring.

Step 1: Establish Governance Structures

- **Board-Level Involvement:**
  Create a dedicated cybersecurity committee or designate board members to oversee security initiatives.

- **Executive Leadership:**
  Appoint a Chief Information Security Officer (CISO) or equivalent to lead governance efforts and serve as a bridge between technical teams and senior management.

- **Define Roles and Responsibilities:**
  Clearly outline the roles of IT, security, legal, and operational teams in managing cybersecurity.

Step 2: Develop and Document Policies

- **Policy Framework:**
  Draft comprehensive cybersecurity policies covering areas such as data protection, incident response, access control, and vendor management.

- **SOPs and Guidelines:**
  Develop detailed procedures that operationalize these

policies, ensuring consistency and clarity in implementation.

- **Periodic Review:**
Establish a schedule for reviewing and updating policies, ensuring they reflect emerging threats and regulatory changes.

Step 3: Integrate Risk Management

- **Risk Assessments:**
Conduct regular risk assessments to identify vulnerabilities and determine the potential impact on the organization.

- **Metrics and Reporting:**
Develop dashboards and reporting tools to communicate risk levels, compliance status, and performance metrics to senior leadership.

- **Feedback Loop:**
Use incident reports and audit findings to refine risk assessments and update policies continuously.

Step 4: Ensure Compliance and Legal Alignment

- **Regulatory Mapping:**
Map out all applicable regulations and standards, ensuring that your governance framework meets these requirements.

- **Audit Programs:**
Implement internal and external audit programs to monitor compliance and enforce accountability.

- **Legal Review:**
Involve legal counsel in policy development and

compliance efforts to mitigate risk and ensure adherence to regulatory obligations.

Step 5: Foster Communication and Training

- **Regular Briefings:**
  Conduct regular security briefings for board members and executive leadership, focusing on current risks, incidents, and strategic initiatives.

- **Employee Training:**
  Implement ongoing training programs to ensure that all employees understand cybersecurity policies and their role in protecting the organization.

- **Engagement Platforms:**
  Use internal portals, newsletters, and feedback sessions to keep cybersecurity at the forefront of organizational culture.

Actionable Task

- **Governance Assessment Exercise:**
  Conduct an organization-wide review of your current cybersecurity governance framework. Develop an inventory of all policies, roles, and reporting mechanisms, then identify one area for improvement— such as establishing a formal cybersecurity committee or updating risk reporting metrics. Draft a plan outlining the changes, include specific metrics (e.g., incident response times), and share the plan with your executive team for feedback.

- **Policy Drafting Exercise:**
  Create a sample cybersecurity policy that outlines key responsibilities, compliance requirements, and risk

management procedures. Ensure the policy includes sections on board involvement, employee training, and continuous improvement. Present the draft to both technical and non-technical stakeholders to gather input and refine the policy.

19.4 Real-World Applications and Case Studies

Case Study 1: Enhancing Governance in a Financial Institution

A mid-sized bank, facing increasing regulatory scrutiny and cyber threats, overhauled its cybersecurity governance framework:

- **Board Engagement:**
  The bank established a cybersecurity committee at the board level, ensuring that senior leadership was directly involved in security strategy.

- **Policy Overhaul:**
  Comprehensive policies were developed and aligned with industry standards such as NIST CSF and ISO 27001.

- **Risk Integration:**
  Regular risk assessments were integrated into the governance framework, with dashboards reporting KPIs like MTTD and MTTR.

- **Outcome:**
  The bank achieved a 50% reduction in security incidents, improved regulatory compliance, and enhanced overall trust among stakeholders.

Case Study 2: Cybersecurity Governance in a Global Manufacturing Company

A global manufacturing company needed to protect both its IT systems and operational technology:

- **Governance Structure:**
  The company implemented a unified governance model that integrated IT and OT security under one framework, with oversight from a dedicated CISO.

- **Policy and Compliance:**
  Policies were updated to meet both cybersecurity and physical safety standards, ensuring seamless compliance with regulations like NERC CIP.

- **Continuous Improvement:**
  Regular audits and cross-functional training sessions led to continuous enhancements in security practices.

- **Outcome:**
  The integrated approach resulted in a 45% improvement in incident response times and a significant reduction in both cyber and physical security breaches.

Global Insight:
A European energy company revamped its cybersecurity governance by integrating risk management with strategic oversight. By aligning cybersecurity investments with business objectives and maintaining rigorous audit procedures, the company set a new industry benchmark for governance excellence, reducing overall risk exposure by 55%.

19.5 Resources and Next Steps

To further strengthen your cybersecurity governance capabilities, consider these resources:

- **Online Courses:**

  - Platforms such as Coursera, Udemy, and Cybrary offer courses on cybersecurity governance, risk management, and compliance.

- **Books:**

  - *"Cybersecurity Governance: Risk Management, Compliance, and Assurance"*

  - *"The Governance of Cybersecurity"*

- **Certifications:**

  - Consider certifications such as Certified Information Systems Auditor (CISA), Certified in Risk and Information Systems Control (CRISC), or CISSP with a focus on governance.

- **Professional Organizations:**

  - Engage with ISACA, (ISC)^2, and the Cloud Security Alliance (CSA) for networking, training, and best practices.

- **Tools:**

  - Explore governance, risk, and compliance (GRC) platforms that help automate policy management, risk assessments, and audit processes.

- **Conferences and Workshops:**

  o Attend events such as the Cybersecurity Leadership Forum or ISACA conferences to stay updated on governance trends and network with industry experts.

Practical Tip:

Start by reviewing your current cybersecurity governance framework. Identify a key gap—such as the lack of regular risk reporting—and develop a plan to address it, incorporating metrics and regular review schedules. Engage stakeholders across the organization to ensure the plan aligns with business objectives.

19.6 Chapter Takeaways

Key Points:

- **Cybersecurity Governance** provides the strategic oversight needed to align security initiatives with business objectives and regulatory requirements.

- Core components include **board and executive involvement, comprehensive policy development, risk management integration, compliance alignment,** and **continuous training and communication.**

- A robust governance framework ensures accountability, fosters a security-aware culture, and supports continuous improvement.

- Real-world case studies demonstrate that effective governance can lead to significant reductions in security incidents and improved regulatory compliance.

- Ongoing evaluation, stakeholder engagement, and adaptation to emerging threats are essential for a resilient governance strategy.

19.7 Test Your Knowledge

1. **Which of the following best describes the primary purpose of cybersecurity governance?**
   A. To manage daily technical configurations
   B. To align security strategies with business objectives and ensure accountability
   C. To replace traditional IT security tools
   D. To automate incident response processes

2. **What is one key benefit of having board-level involvement in cybersecurity governance?**
   A. It reduces the need for technical controls
   B. It ensures that cybersecurity initiatives receive strategic oversight and proper funding
   C. It simplifies network configurations
   D. It eliminates the need for risk assessments

3. **Scenario Question:**
   Imagine you are a cybersecurity manager at a multinational corporation. Describe one strategy you would implement to improve cybersecurity governance (e.g., establishing a dedicated cybersecurity committee) and explain how you would measure its effectiveness. Include specific tools or metrics that might be used.

4. **Reflective Exercise:**
   Draw a simplified diagram of your organization's cybersecurity governance structure, including key roles, reporting lines, and decision-making processes.

Identify one potential gap in this structure and propose an improvement. Outline how you would communicate these changes to both technical staff and the board.

19.8 Final Thoughts

Cybersecurity governance is a critical pillar of an effective cyber defense strategy. It ensures that security efforts are aligned with business objectives, regulatory requirements, and risk management practices. This chapter has provided a detailed exploration of the essential components of cybersecurity governance, practical steps for implementation, and real-world case studies that highlight the benefits of a robust governance framework.

As you continue your journey through this book, the principles of governance will intertwine with other core areas—such as risk management, network security, and incident response—to form a cohesive, resilient defense strategy. Continuous improvement, stakeholder engagement, and a proactive approach to policy and compliance are essential to maintaining a strong cybersecurity posture in today's ever-evolving threat landscape.

Thank you for exploring Chapter 19. Apply these insights and actionable tasks to enhance your cybersecurity governance framework, and continue your journey toward mastering a strategic, integrated cyber defense approach.

End of Chapter 19

Global cyber laws and ethics establish the legal and moral frameworks that govern behavior in the digital domain. As cyber threats transcend borders, organizations must navigate a complex landscape of regulations and ethical considerations to ensure that their security practices are both legally compliant and morally sound. In this chapter, we explore the key international laws, standards, and ethical issues related to cybersecurity. Building on the governance, compliance, and risk management concepts discussed in earlier chapters, you will learn how to interpret and apply global cyber laws, address ethical dilemmas, and implement strategies that balance security with individual rights and corporate responsibility.

Expert Insight:
"Cyber laws and ethics are not only about enforcing rules— they're about shaping a secure and just digital environment that respects privacy, fosters trust, and supports innovation across borders." — Global Cyber Law Expert

20.1 What Are Global Cyber Laws and Ethics?

Global cyber laws encompass the international, national, and regional regulations designed to protect information, privacy, and critical infrastructure in the digital world. These laws address issues ranging from data protection and privacy to cybercrime and state-sponsored cyber activities. Cyber ethics, on the other hand, involves the moral principles and values that guide behavior in cyberspace. Together, they ensure that actions in the digital realm are legally compliant and ethically responsible.

Key objectives include:

- **Protecting Privacy:** Ensuring that personal data is handled with respect and protected from unauthorized access.

- **Defining Cyber Crime:** Establishing legal boundaries to prosecute cybercriminals and deter illegal activities.

- **Regulating State Actions:** Setting standards for state-sponsored cyber operations and international cooperation.

- **Balancing Innovation and Security:** Creating an environment that encourages technological progress while safeguarding rights and interests.

The interplay between laws and ethics in cybersecurity is complex. While regulations provide clear legal guidelines, ethical considerations often extend beyond legal obligations, addressing issues of fairness, transparency, and accountability.

20.2 Core Components of Global Cyber Laws and Ethics

A robust understanding of global cyber laws and ethics involves several key components:

International Regulations and Frameworks

- **United Nations Conventions:**
  International efforts such as the Budapest Convention on Cybercrime provide a framework for cooperation in investigating and prosecuting cybercrime.

- **Regional Regulations:**
  Regulations like the European Union's General Data Protection Regulation (GDPR) set high standards for data privacy and protection, influencing global practices.

- **National Cyber Laws:**
  Countries develop their own laws (e.g., the U.S. Computer Fraud and Abuse Act, China's Cybersecurity Law) to address cybercrime, digital privacy, and cybersecurity responsibilities.

Data Protection and Privacy

- **Legal Requirements:**
  Global data protection laws, such as GDPR, mandate that organizations implement strict measures to safeguard personal information.

- **Ethical Considerations:**
  Beyond legal compliance, ethical data handling involves transparency, user consent, and respecting individual privacy rights.

Cybercrime and Criminal Liability

- **Defining Cybercrime:**
  Laws outline what constitutes illegal activities in cyberspace, including hacking, identity theft, and the distribution of malware.

- **Jurisdictional Challenges:**
  Cybercrime often spans multiple countries, complicating legal enforcement and necessitating international cooperation.

- **Ethical Implications:**
  Ethical questions arise regarding surveillance, privacy intrusions, and the balance between security and civil liberties.

State-Sponsored Cyber Activities and International Norms

- **Cyber Warfare:**
  International law is still evolving to address state-sponsored cyber-attacks and cyber espionage.

- **Diplomatic Engagement:**
  Efforts to establish international norms and treaties aim to regulate state behavior in cyberspace.

- **Ethical Dilemmas:**
  Balancing national security interests with global stability and human rights is a major ethical challenge.

Corporate Responsibility and Compliance

- **Governance Requirements:**
  Organizations must align their cybersecurity practices with legal standards while adhering to ethical guidelines.

- **Compliance Programs:**
  Regular audits, risk assessments, and policy updates ensure ongoing adherence to laws and regulations.

- **Ethical Corporate Conduct:**
  Beyond compliance, companies are increasingly expected to operate transparently and ethically, fostering trust with customers and stakeholders.

20.3 Implementing Global Cyber Laws and Ethics

Implementing a comprehensive framework for global cyber laws and ethics involves a strategic, multi-step approach:

Step 1: Regulatory Assessment and Gap Analysis

- **Inventory of Legal Obligations:**
  Identify all applicable cyber laws and regulations based on your organization's location and the regions in which it operates.

- **Gap Analysis:**
  Compare your current cybersecurity policies and practices against regulatory requirements and ethical best practices. Identify gaps that need to be addressed.

- **Risk Prioritization:**
  Prioritize gaps based on potential legal penalties, reputational damage, and ethical concerns.

Step 2: Policy Development and Enforcement

- **Drafting Policies:**
  Develop comprehensive cybersecurity policies that incorporate both legal mandates and ethical principles. Ensure policies cover data protection, incident reporting, access controls, and employee conduct.

- **Legal and Ethical Review:**
  Involve legal counsel and ethics committees to review policies, ensuring they are both compliant and morally sound.

- **Enforcement Mechanisms:**
  Establish clear procedures and accountability
  structures to enforce policies, including regular audits
  and compliance checks.

Step 3: Integration with Security Programs

- **Risk Management Integration:**
  Incorporate legal and ethical considerations into risk
  assessments and incident response plans.

- **Training Programs:**
  Educate employees on the legal and ethical dimensions
  of cybersecurity. Include case studies, real-world
  examples, and role-specific training.

- **Technology Alignment:**
  Ensure that your cybersecurity tools, such as SIEM
  systems and data loss prevention solutions, are
  configured to support compliance with regulatory
  standards.

Step 4: Continuous Monitoring and Improvement

- **Audit Programs:**
  Regularly audit your cybersecurity practices and
  policies to ensure ongoing compliance with evolving
  laws and ethical standards.

- **Feedback Mechanisms:**
  Establish channels for stakeholders to provide
  feedback on policies and report concerns regarding
  ethical conduct.

- **Updates and Revisions:**
  Stay informed about changes in international, national,

and regional cyber laws, and update your policies and practices accordingly.

Step 5: Stakeholder Engagement and Reporting

- **Board and Executive Reporting:**
  Regularly report on compliance, risk assessments, and policy updates to senior leadership and the board.

- **Transparency:**
  Maintain transparency with customers, regulators, and the public about your cybersecurity practices and ethical commitments.

- **Collaboration:**
  Engage in industry groups and information-sharing communities to stay current on best practices and contribute to shaping global cyber norms.

Actionable Task

- **Governance and Ethics Audit:**
  Conduct an internal audit to review your current cybersecurity policies and practices against applicable global cyber laws and ethical standards. Document areas where your practices meet or exceed requirements and identify gaps needing improvement. Draft a report outlining these findings along with a remediation plan that includes specific timelines and accountability measures. Share the report with senior management and incorporate feedback for continuous improvement.

- **Policy Drafting Exercise:**
  Create a sample policy that integrates both legal and ethical considerations for data handling. For example,

include provisions for transparent data collection, secure storage, and clear user consent protocols. Circulate the draft among legal, IT, and HR departments for input and refinement.

20.4 Real-World Applications and Case Studies

Case Study 1: A Global Financial Institution's Compliance Overhaul

A multinational bank, operating across multiple jurisdictions, needed to harmonize its cybersecurity practices with diverse legal requirements:

- **Regulatory Mapping:**
  The bank mapped its operations to applicable regulations such as GDPR, the U.S. Computer Fraud and Abuse Act, and regional data protection laws.

- **Policy Integration:**
  Comprehensive policies were developed to integrate these requirements with ethical practices—ensuring data transparency, user consent, and strict access controls.

- **Audit and Reporting:**
  Regular audits and robust reporting mechanisms ensured ongoing compliance and allowed the bank to proactively address regulatory changes.

- **Outcome:**
  The bank reduced non-compliance risks by 50% and enhanced stakeholder trust, setting a benchmark for global cyber governance.

Case Study 2: Cyber Ethics in a Technology Firm

A leading technology firm faced public scrutiny over its handling of user data and privacy concerns:

- **Ethical Framework Development:**
  The firm developed an ethical framework that went beyond legal compliance to address transparency, accountability, and user rights.

- **Policy and Training:**
  Comprehensive policies were implemented, accompanied by mandatory training sessions that educated employees on ethical data handling practices.

- **Stakeholder Engagement:**
  Regular public reports and open forums were established to communicate the firm's ethical commitments and gather feedback.

- **Outcome:**
  The initiative not only improved regulatory compliance but also restored public confidence and strengthened the firm's reputation as a responsible corporate citizen.

Global Insight:
A European energy company, operating under strict regulatory environments, integrated cyber laws with ethical guidelines to create a resilient governance framework. Their proactive approach led to a 55% reduction in security incidents and positioned them as leaders in global cyber ethics.

20.5 Resources and Next Steps

To further your understanding and implementation of global cyber laws and ethics, consider the following resources:

- **Online Courses:**

    o Platforms like Coursera, Udemy, and Cybrary offer courses on cybersecurity law, compliance, and ethical frameworks.

- **Books:**

    o *"Cybersecurity and Cyberlaw: A Global Perspective"*

    o *"Ethics and the Law in Cybersecurity"*

- **Certifications:**

    o Consider certifications such as Certified Information Privacy Professional (CIPP) or Certified Information Systems Auditor (CISA) with a focus on cyber governance.

- **Professional Organizations:**

    o Engage with ISACA, (ISC)^2, and the International Association of Privacy Professionals (IAPP) for training, webinars, and networking opportunities.

- **Tools and Platforms:**

    o Explore Governance, Risk, and Compliance (GRC) platforms that streamline policy management, risk assessments, and audit processes.

- **Conferences and Workshops:**
    - Attend events like the Cybersecurity Leadership Forum or ISACA conferences to stay updated on emerging legal trends and ethical challenges.

Practical Tip:
Begin by conducting a comprehensive review of your organization's current cybersecurity policies and regulatory compliance status. Identify key gaps and develop a prioritized remediation plan. Engage stakeholders across departments to ensure that policy updates are both legally compliant and ethically sound.

20.6 Chapter Takeaways

Key Points:

- **Global Cyber Laws and Ethics** provide the legal and moral framework for cybersecurity, ensuring that organizations operate responsibly and in compliance with international, national, and regional regulations.

- Core components include **international and national cyber laws, data protection and privacy, cybercrime definitions, state-sponsored cyber activities,** and **corporate governance.**

- Effective implementation requires a structured approach: conducting regulatory assessments, developing comprehensive policies, integrating risk management, and fostering transparent communication.

- Real-world case studies illustrate how robust governance frameworks can reduce non-compliance risks and build trust among stakeholders.

- Continuous monitoring, stakeholder engagement, and adaptation to emerging legal and ethical challenges are essential to maintaining a resilient cybersecurity posture.

20.7 Test Your Knowledge

1. **Which of the following best describes the primary purpose of global cyber laws?**
   A. To manage technical configurations in an organization
   B. To establish legal frameworks that protect digital assets and ensure compliance across borders
   C. To automate network security operations
   D. To replace traditional encryption methods

2. **What is one key benefit of integrating ethical considerations into cybersecurity governance?**
   A. It simplifies the legal framework
   B. It enhances transparency and builds trust with stakeholders
   C. It reduces the need for technical controls
   D. It minimizes employee training requirements

3. **Scenario Question:**
   Imagine you are a cybersecurity manager at a multinational corporation. Describe one strategy you would implement to ensure your organization complies with global cyber laws (e.g., GDPR, CCPA) while upholding ethical standards in data handling. Include

specific tools or methodologies and explain how you would measure the strategy's success.

4. **Reflective Exercise:**
   Create a simplified diagram of your organization's cybersecurity governance structure, including key roles, policies, and compliance processes. Identify one potential gap related to legal or ethical challenges and propose an improvement. Outline how you would communicate this change to both technical staff and senior management.

20.8 Final Thoughts

Global cyber laws and ethics are critical to building a secure and responsible digital environment. By establishing clear legal frameworks and embedding ethical considerations into cybersecurity governance, organizations can navigate complex regulatory landscapes, protect individual privacy, and foster trust among stakeholders. This chapter has provided a comprehensive exploration of international, national, and regional cyber laws, along with the ethical challenges that shape our digital world. Through real-world case studies and actionable tasks, you now have the tools to assess and enhance your organization's governance framework.

As you continue your journey through this book, the principles discussed here will integrate with other core areas—such as risk management, network security, and incident response—to form a cohesive, robust cyber defense strategy. Continuous improvement, proactive engagement, and a commitment to ethical conduct are essential to staying ahead in today's dynamic threat landscape.

Thank you for exploring Chapter 20. Apply these insights and tasks to refine your cybersecurity governance, ensuring that your organization not only complies with global standards but also upholds the highest ethical principles in its operations.

End of Chapter 20

Third-party and supply chain risk management is an essential aspect of cybersecurity governance that addresses the vulnerabilities introduced by external vendors, service providers, and supply chain partners. In today's interconnected world, organizations must extend their security measures beyond their internal networks to ensure that external dependencies do not become entry points for cyber threats. This chapter explores the key concepts, methodologies, and best practices for managing third-party and supply chain risks. Drawing on frameworks and risk management principles discussed in earlier chapters, you will learn how to assess, monitor, and mitigate risks originating from external sources. Real-world case studies and actionable tasks provide practical insights for building a resilient supply chain security strategy.

Expert Insight:
"No organization is an island. Third-party and supply chain risks can be the weakest link in your cybersecurity posture. Managing these risks is critical to ensuring that your overall defense is as strong as your internal measures." — Cybersecurity Risk Management Expert

---

21.1 What Is Third-Party and Supply Chain Risk?

Third-party and supply chain risk refers to the potential vulnerabilities and threats introduced through relationships with external vendors, partners, and service providers. These risks can arise from:

- **Vendor Security Practices:** Weak security controls at a vendor's organization that can be exploited.

- **Interconnected Systems:** The integration of third-party software or hardware that may have undiscovered vulnerabilities.

- **Supply Chain Compromises:** Attacks that target the supply chain—such as software updates or hardware components—leading to widespread exposure.

- **Operational Dependencies:** Critical processes that rely on external entities, where disruptions can impact business continuity.

Managing these risks requires a comprehensive approach that not only assesses the security posture of external partners but also implements controls to mitigate the impact of potential breaches.

21.2 Core Components of Third-Party and Supply Chain Risk Management

A robust strategy for managing third-party and supply chain risk involves several key components:

Vendor Risk Assessment

- **Initial Evaluation:**
  Assess potential vendors' cybersecurity practices before onboarding. This includes reviewing their security certifications, audit reports, and compliance with industry standards.

- **Ongoing Monitoring:**
  Continuously evaluate vendors' performance through regular assessments, vulnerability scans, and security questionnaires.

Contractual and Legal Protections

- **Security Clauses:**
  Include specific cybersecurity requirements, data protection mandates, and incident reporting obligations in contracts.

- **Liability and Indemnification:**
  Define responsibilities and liabilities for breaches or security failures.

- **Compliance Requirements:**
  Ensure that vendors adhere to relevant regulations (e.g., GDPR, HIPAA) and industry standards.

Supply Chain Mapping and Analysis

- **Asset Mapping:**
  Create a comprehensive map of your supply chain, identifying all critical suppliers, partners, and third-party services.

- **Risk Prioritization:**
  Use risk matrices to classify suppliers based on their potential impact on your operations. Focus on those handling sensitive data or providing critical services.

Integration of Threat Intelligence

- **External Intelligence:**
  Leverage threat intelligence feeds that provide insights

into vulnerabilities and threats affecting suppliers and third parties.

- **Collaboration:**
  Participate in industry-specific information-sharing communities to exchange insights and best practices with peers.

Continuous Monitoring and Auditing

- **Regular Audits:**
  Schedule periodic audits of third-party security practices to ensure ongoing compliance.

- **Automated Tools:**
  Use tools that integrate with your SIEM to monitor external access and detect anomalies related to third-party interactions.

- **Incident Response Coordination:**
  Ensure that your incident response plan includes procedures for handling breaches involving third parties.

21.3 Implementing Third-Party and Supply Chain Risk Management

Deploying an effective third-party risk management strategy requires a structured, multi-phase approach:

Step 1: Conduct a Comprehensive Inventory

- **Asset Inventory:**
  Compile a detailed list of all vendors, partners, and

suppliers. Document the types of services they provide and the data they access.

- **Supply Chain Mapping:**
  Develop visual maps to understand interdependencies and identify critical nodes within the supply chain.

Step 2: Perform Vendor Risk Assessments

- **Initial Screening:**
  Evaluate each vendor's cybersecurity posture using questionnaires, security audits, and industry certifications.

- **Ongoing Evaluation:**
  Set up periodic reviews and continuous monitoring to detect any changes in vendor security practices.

- **Risk Scoring:**
  Use a risk matrix to assign scores based on factors such as data sensitivity, operational impact, and historical performance.

Step 3: Develop and Enforce Contracts and Policies

- **Contractual Requirements:**
  Embed robust security clauses in vendor contracts. Specify requirements for regular security audits, incident reporting, and compliance with relevant standards.

- **Internal Policies:**
  Develop internal policies that define how third-party risks are managed and integrated into your overall cybersecurity strategy.

- **Compliance Checks:**
  Ensure that vendors meet your organization's security standards and regulatory requirements before and during their engagement.

Step 4: Integrate Threat Intelligence and Continuous Monitoring

- **Threat Intelligence Integration:**
  Incorporate external threat feeds and intelligence reports to monitor potential vulnerabilities affecting your supply chain.

- **Automated Monitoring:**
  Use SIEM integration and specialized monitoring tools to track third-party activities and identify unusual behaviors or access patterns.

- **Incident Response Coordination:**
  Include third-party risk scenarios in your incident response plan to ensure swift action in the event of a breach.

Step 5: Training, Communication, and Improvement

- **Stakeholder Training:**
  Train internal teams on the importance of third-party risk management, including how to assess vendor security and respond to supply chain incidents.

- **Feedback Mechanisms:**
  Establish channels for feedback from both internal teams and vendors to continuously improve risk management practices.

- **Regular Updates:**
  Stay current with evolving threats and regulatory changes by updating policies and risk assessments periodically.

Actionable Task

- **Vendor Risk Inventory Exercise:**
  Develop a comprehensive inventory of all third-party vendors and suppliers. For each, assign a risk score based on data sensitivity, operational impact, and past performance. Identify one high-risk vendor and create a detailed remediation plan that includes specific contractual updates, continuous monitoring tools, and scheduled audits. Present your findings and plan to your risk management team for review.

- **Policy Drafting Exercise:**
  Draft a sample third-party risk management policy that outlines vendor evaluation criteria, contractual obligations, monitoring requirements, and incident response procedures. Ensure the policy includes sections on compliance, data protection, and communication protocols. Share this draft with legal, IT, and procurement teams for feedback and refinement.

21.4 Real-World Applications and Case Studies

Case Study 1: Financial Institution Strengthens Supply Chain Security

A mid-sized bank recognized that its reliance on several third-party vendors was creating potential vulnerabilities:

- **Vendor Assessment:**
  The bank conducted comprehensive risk assessments of its vendors, identifying those with access to critical customer data.

- **Contractual Enhancements:**
  New contracts were established with stringent cybersecurity requirements, including regular audits and compliance with GDPR.

- **Continuous Monitoring:**
  Integration of vendor logs into the bank's SIEM allowed for real-time monitoring and early detection of anomalies.

- **Outcome:**
  The bank achieved a 50% reduction in third-party related incidents and bolstered overall trust among stakeholders.

Case Study 2: Global Manufacturing Company Mitigates Supply Chain Risks

A global manufacturing firm, heavily dependent on a complex supply chain, faced risks from suppliers providing critical components:

- **Supply Chain Mapping:**
  The company mapped out its entire supply chain and identified critical nodes.

- **Risk-Based Prioritization:**
  Vendors were scored based on their impact on production and data sensitivity. High-risk suppliers were subjected to more rigorous audits and enhanced contractual obligations.

- **Threat Intelligence and Collaboration:**
  The company integrated external threat intelligence feeds to monitor vulnerabilities affecting its suppliers and participated in industry-specific information-sharing communities.

- **Outcome:**
  The initiative resulted in a 45% reduction in supply chain-related vulnerabilities and improved overall production reliability.

Global Insight:
A European technology firm, operating across multiple countries, integrated advanced third-party risk management practices. By establishing standardized security requirements and continuous monitoring of its supply chain, the firm reduced potential attack vectors by 55% and set a new benchmark for international supply chain security.

21.5 Resources and Next Steps

To further enhance your third-party and supply chain risk management capabilities, consider these resources:

- **Books:**

  - *"Supply Chain Risk Management: Vulnerability and Resilience in Logistics"*

  - *"Third-Party Risk Management in Cybersecurity"*

- **Certifications:**

  - Consider certifications such as Certified Third-Party Risk Professional (CTPRP) or Certified

Information Systems Auditor (CISA) with a focus on supply chain risk.

- **Professional Organizations:**
  - Engage with ISACA, (ISC)^2, and the Global Supply Chain Institute for networking, training, and best practices.

- **Tools and Platforms:**
  - Explore Governance, Risk, and Compliance (GRC) platforms that support third-party risk assessments and continuous monitoring.

- **Conferences and Workshops:**
  - Attend events such as the Supply Chain Risk Management Conference or cybersecurity leadership forums to stay updated on emerging trends and practices.

Practical Tip:
Begin by conducting a third-party risk assessment for your most critical suppliers. Use the results to update contractual requirements and integrate automated monitoring tools. Establish a routine review process to keep your risk assessments current.

21.6 Chapter Takeaways

Key Points:

- **Third-Party and Supply Chain Risk Management** focuses on identifying, assessing, and mitigating risks introduced by external vendors and partners.

- Core components include **vendor risk assessments, contractual and legal protections, supply chain mapping, threat intelligence integration,** and **continuous monitoring.**

- A structured approach involves a comprehensive inventory, risk assessments, policy development, deployment of monitoring tools, and regular audits.

- Real-world case studies show that effective supply chain risk management can reduce vulnerabilities by up to 50–55%, ensuring operational continuity and regulatory compliance.

- Continuous improvement through stakeholder training, updated policies, and adaptive monitoring is essential to manage evolving risks.

21.7 Test Your Knowledge

1. **Which of the following best describes the primary objective of vendor risk assessments?**
   A. To increase network speed
   B. To evaluate and monitor the security posture of external suppliers
   C. To simplify the onboarding process
   D. To automate software updates

2. **What is one key benefit of using a Governance, Risk, and Compliance (GRC) platform for third-party risk management?**
   A. It eliminates the need for contracts
   B. It streamlines the assessment, monitoring, and reporting of vendor risks

C. It replaces the need for internal audits

D. It increases the number of suppliers

3. **Scenario Question:**
Imagine you are the cybersecurity manager for a multinational corporation. Describe one strategy you would implement to mitigate supply chain risks associated with critical vendors and explain how you would measure its effectiveness. Include specific tools or methodologies in your answer.

4. **Reflective Exercise:**
Draw a simplified diagram of your organization's supply chain, identifying key vendors and potential risk points. For each risk point, propose one mitigation strategy and outline how you would update your security policies to address these risks. Explain how you would communicate these changes to both technical staff and senior management.

21.8 Final Thoughts

Third-party and supply chain risk management is a critical component of a comprehensive cybersecurity strategy. By systematically assessing vendor risks, establishing robust contractual protections, and continuously monitoring the security posture of external partners, organizations can mitigate potential vulnerabilities and protect their operational integrity. This chapter has provided a detailed overview of the strategies, tools, and best practices necessary to manage these risks effectively. Real-world case studies illustrate that with a proactive approach, organizations can significantly reduce supply chain vulnerabilities and enhance overall security.

As you continue your journey through this book, the principles discussed here will integrate with other core areas—such as risk management, cybersecurity governance, and technical defenses—to create a cohesive and resilient cyber defense framework. Continuous evaluation, collaboration with vendors, and a commitment to ongoing improvement are essential to managing the evolving risks in today's interconnected world.

Thank you for exploring Chapter 21. Apply these insights and actionable tasks to strengthen your third-party and supply chain risk management practices and continue your journey toward mastering cyber defense.

End of Chapter 21

Part 5: Case Studies and Real-World Lessons

Chapter 22: High-Profile Cyber Attacks

High-profile cyber-attacks capture global headlines and serve as critical learning opportunities for the cybersecurity community. These incidents, often targeting major corporations, government agencies, or critical infrastructure, reveal vulnerabilities in systems that can have widespread consequences. In this chapter, we explore notable cyber-attacks, analyze the tactics used by adversaries, and discuss the lessons learned from these events. By studying these high-profile cases, you'll gain insights into the evolving threat landscape and understand how to fortify your defenses against similar attacks.

Expert Insight:
"Every high-profile attack is a wake-up call—a demonstration of what can go wrong when vulnerabilities are exploited at scale. Studying these incidents helps us build a more resilient and proactive defense." — Cybersecurity Incident Response Leader

---

22.1 Understanding High-Profile Cyber Attacks

High-profile cyber-attacks are incidents that attract significant media and public attention due to their scale, impact, or the notoriety of the targets. They typically involve sophisticated tactics and exploit multiple vulnerabilities, leading to substantial financial, operational, or reputational damage.

266

Key characteristics include:

- **Wide Impact:** Affecting millions of users or entire sectors.

- **Advanced Techniques:** Utilizing sophisticated methods such as ransomware, phishing, or supply chain compromises.

- **Significant Consequences:** Leading to financial losses, regulatory penalties, and erosion of public trust.

- **Rapid Evolution:** Demonstrating the evolving nature of cyber threats and the need for continuous improvement in defenses.

These attacks serve as case studies that provide invaluable lessons for enhancing cyber defenses and developing effective incident response strategies.

22.2 Notable Case Studies

Analyzing real-world attacks helps illustrate how adversaries operate and what defenses may have mitigated the incidents. Below are detailed overviews of several high-profile cyber-attacks.

Case Study 1: WannaCry Ransomware Attack (2017)

- **Overview:**
  WannaCry was a global ransomware attack that exploited a vulnerability in outdated Windows systems using the EternalBlue exploit.

- **Attack Vector:**
  The ransomware spread rapidly across networks, encrypting files and demanding Bitcoin payments.

- **Impact:**
  Major disruptions were seen in sectors such as healthcare, where hospitals experienced severe operational setbacks, along with significant financial losses worldwide.

- **Lessons Learned:**

  - **Patch Management:** Timely software updates are critical.

  - **Network Segmentation:** Isolating systems can limit lateral movement of ransomware.

  - **Backup Strategies:** Regular, secure backups enable swift recovery.

Case Study 2: Equifax Data Breach (2017)

- **Overview:**
  The Equifax breach exposed sensitive personal data of approximately 150 million individuals, resulting from an unpatched vulnerability in a web application.

- **Attack Vector:**
  Exploitation of a known vulnerability allowed attackers to bypass security controls and access vast amounts of personal information.

- **Impact:**
  The breach led to significant financial losses, legal ramifications, and a long-lasting erosion of consumer trust.

- **Lessons Learned:**

  o **Vulnerability Management:** Continuous monitoring and prompt patching are essential.

  o **Access Controls:** Strict access management could have limited the exposure of sensitive data.

  o **Risk Assessment:** Regular risk assessments help identify and mitigate potential vulnerabilities.

Case Study 3: SolarWinds Supply Chain Attack (2020)

- **Overview:**
  The SolarWinds attack was a sophisticated supply chain compromise where attackers inserted malicious code into a software update.

- **Attack Vector:**
  The compromised update was distributed to thousands of SolarWinds customers, enabling attackers to infiltrate numerous high-profile organizations, including government agencies.

- **Impact:**
  The breach exposed sensitive data and raised significant concerns about the security of supply chain processes.

- **Lessons Learned:**

  o **Supply Chain Security:** Rigorous vetting and continuous monitoring of third-party software are crucial.

  o **Incident Response:** A coordinated and timely response can limit the impact of widespread breaches.

o **Zero Trust Architecture:** Implementing a Zero Trust model could have reduced the attackers' lateral movement.

Case Study 4: Colonial Pipeline Ransomware Attack (2021)

- **Overview:**
  The Colonial Pipeline attack disrupted fuel supplies across the eastern United States by encrypting critical operational systems.

- **Attack Vector:**
  Ransomware compromised the network through vulnerable endpoints, leading to the shutdown of pipeline operations.

- **Impact:**
  The incident resulted in fuel shortages, price spikes, and highlighted vulnerabilities in critical infrastructure.

- **Lessons Learned:**

  o **Critical Infrastructure Protection:** Enhanced monitoring and segmentation of critical systems are essential.

  o **Incident Preparedness:** A well-practiced incident response plan can minimize downtime and impact.

  o **Collaboration:** Effective communication between public and private sectors is vital during crisis response.

22.3 Lessons Learned from High-Profile Cyber Attacks

Studying these attacks provides several critical lessons that can be applied across organizations:

Importance of Continuous Monitoring

- **Detection and Response:**
  High-profile attacks often go undetected for extended periods. Continuous monitoring with tools like SIEM and EDR is vital for early detection and rapid response.

Robust Patch Management and Vulnerability Assessment

- **Timeliness:**
  Regular vulnerability assessments and prompt patching can prevent attackers from exploiting known vulnerabilities.

- **Proactive Measures:**
  Integrating automated vulnerability scanning into daily operations can help identify weaknesses before they are exploited.

Need for Network Segmentation and Zero Trust

- **Containment:**
  Isolating critical systems through network segmentation limits lateral movement, reducing the overall impact of a breach.

- **Verification:**
  A Zero Trust model, where every access request is verified, can further enhance defense against sophisticated attacks.

Strengthening Supply Chain Security

- **Third-Party Risk:**
  High-profile supply chain attacks, like SolarWinds, underscore the need for rigorous third-party risk management and continuous monitoring of vendor software and hardware.

- **Collaboration:**
  Sharing threat intelligence and best practices among industry peers strengthens overall security.

Comprehensive Incident Response

- **Preparation and Drills:**
  Effective incident response plans, backed by regular drills and simulations, can drastically reduce recovery times and mitigate damage.

- **Cross-Functional Coordination:**
  Coordination between IT, security, legal, and communication teams is essential for an effective response.

22.4 Implementing Lessons in Your Organization

Integrating lessons from high-profile attacks into your cybersecurity strategy involves several practical steps:

Step 1: Enhance Monitoring and Alerting

- **Deploy Advanced SIEM:**
  Ensure that your SIEM system is configured to collect logs from all critical systems and alert on anomalous behavior.

- **Implement EDR Solutions:**
  Use Endpoint Detection and Response tools to continuously monitor for unusual activities at the endpoint level.

Step 2: Strengthen Patch and Vulnerability Management

- **Automate Scanning:**
  Integrate automated vulnerability scanners to conduct regular assessments.

- **Patch Management:**
  Establish a robust patch management process to ensure timely updates.

Step 3: Revise Network Architecture

- **Segment Networks:**
  Implement network segmentation to isolate critical systems.

- **Adopt Zero Trust:**
  Gradually transition to a Zero Trust model, ensuring that every access request is continuously verified.

Step 4: Review and Update Incident Response Plans

- **Conduct Drills:**
  Regularly test your incident response plan with simulations that mimic high-profile attack scenarios.

- **Post-Incident Analysis:**
  After each drill or actual incident, perform a thorough review to identify improvements.

Actionable Task

- **Cyber Attack Simulation Exercise:**
  Organize a simulated attack scenario modeled after a high-profile incident (e.g., a ransomware attack or supply chain breach). Document each phase—from initial detection to response and recovery. Measure key metrics such as detection time and recovery time and identify any gaps in your current defenses. Prepare a report with recommendations for improvement and present it to your incident response team.

- **Vendor Security Review:**
  Conduct a detailed review of your third-party and supply chain security measures. Identify one high-risk vendor or software component and develop a plan to enhance its security, incorporating lessons from high-profile attacks. Include measures such as enhanced monitoring, stricter contractual requirements, and regular audits.

22.5 Resources and Next Steps

To further your understanding of high-profile cyber-attacks and how to mitigate similar risks, consider these resources:

- **Online Courses:**

  - Platforms like Coursera, Udemy, and Cybrary offer courses on advanced threat detection, incident response, and cybersecurity risk management.

- **Books:**

  - *"The Art of Invisibility"* by Kevin Mitnick

  - *"Cyber War: The Next Threat to National Security and What to Do About It"*

- **Certifications:**

  - Consider certifications such as Certified Information Systems Security Professional (CISSP) or Certified Ethical Hacker (CEH) to deepen your expertise.

- **Professional Organizations:**

  - Engage with organizations like the SANS Institute, (ISC)², and ISACA for the latest research, case studies, and networking opportunities.

- **Tools:**

  - Experiment with open-source tools like Metasploit, Burp Suite, and various SIEM platforms to simulate attacks and analyze their impact.

- **Conferences and Workshops:**

  - Attend events such as DEF CON, Black Hat, or regional cybersecurity summits to stay informed about emerging threats and defensive strategies.

Practical Tip:
Start by setting up a test environment where you can safely simulate high-profile attack scenarios. Use this environment to

evaluate your current detection and response capabilities, then iteratively refine your processes based on your findings.

22.6 Chapter Takeaways

Key Points:

- **High-Profile Cyber Attacks** illustrate the evolving and sophisticated nature of modern threats, highlighting the vulnerabilities in large-scale systems.

- Studying these attacks provides critical insights into the tactics, techniques, and procedures used by adversaries.

- Key lessons include the importance of continuous monitoring, robust patch management, network segmentation, and comprehensive incident response.

- Real-world case studies demonstrate that proactive measures can significantly reduce the impact of cyber-attacks, with some organizations achieving up to a 50% reduction in incidents.

- Implementing lessons learned from high-profile attacks involves enhancing monitoring, revising network architectures, and continuously testing and updating incident response plans.

- Collaboration, information sharing, and continuous improvement are essential to staying ahead of emerging threats.

22.7 Test Your Knowledge

1. **Which of the following is a common characteristic of high-profile cyber-attacks?**
   A. They are usually minor and localized incidents.
   B. They often involve advanced tactics and affect large numbers of users or critical systems.
   C. They are solely caused by insider threats.
   D. They are typically easily mitigated with basic antivirus software.

2. **What is one key lesson learned from the SolarWinds supply chain attack?**
   A. The importance of robust third-party risk management
   B. The need for faster Wi-Fi connections
   C. That only government agencies are at risk
   D. That encryption is unnecessary

3. **Scenario Question:**
   Imagine you are a cybersecurity manager at a large enterprise. You need to prepare for a potential ransomware attack similar to WannaCry. Describe one strategy you would implement to mitigate the risk and minimize downtime and explain how you would measure its success. Include specific tools or processes in your answer.

4. **Reflective Exercise:**
   Draw a simplified diagram of a high-profile cyber attack's lifecycle, from initial intrusion to incident response and recovery. Identify one critical failure point in the attack chain and propose a mitigation strategy. Explain how you would test this mitigation and communicate the results to your leadership team.

22.8 Final Thoughts

High-profile cyber-attacks serve as stark reminders of the vulnerabilities inherent in our interconnected digital world. By studying these incidents, organizations can glean valuable lessons on effective threat detection, robust incident response, and continuous improvement. This chapter has provided a detailed exploration of notable cyber-attacks, the tactics employed by adversaries, and the key lessons that can be applied to strengthen your security posture.

As you continue your journey through this book, the insights from high-profile attacks will integrate with other core areas— such as risk management, network security, and incident response—to form a comprehensive, resilient cyber defense framework. By continuously learning from past incidents and adapting your strategies, you can build a proactive security environment that is prepared to face the evolving threat landscape.

Thank you for exploring Chapter 22. Apply these insights and actionable tasks to enhance your defenses against high-profile cyber-attacks and continue your journey toward mastering cyber defense.

End of Chapter 22

Cyber threats manifest differently across industries due to unique operational environments, regulatory requirements, and technology stacks. In this chapter, we explore industry-specific scenarios that illustrate the diverse challenges organizations face. By analyzing case studies from sectors such as healthcare, finance, retail, energy, and manufacturing, you will gain insights into tailored defense strategies. Building on the core principles of cyber defense discussed in previous chapters, this chapter emphasizes the need for customized security measures that address sector-specific risks. Real-world examples and actionable tasks will guide you in applying these lessons within your own industry.

Expert Insight:
"Understanding the nuances of cyber threats in specific industries is crucial. A one-size-fits-all approach rarely works—security strategies must be tailored to the unique risks and regulatory landscapes of each sector." — Industry Cybersecurity Specialist

23.1 What Are Industry-Specific Scenarios?

Industry-specific scenarios refer to the distinct types of cyber-attacks, vulnerabilities, and security challenges that organizations encounter within particular sectors. Each industry faces unique risks based on the nature of its data, operational technologies, and external dependencies. For instance:

- **Healthcare:** Attacks may target patient records and medical devices, leading to both privacy breaches and potential harm to patient safety.

- **Finance:** Cyber criminals may focus on stealing financial data, committing fraud, or disrupting financial transactions.

- **Retail:** Point-of-sale (POS) systems and e-commerce platforms are frequent targets for data breaches and payment fraud.

- **Energy and Utilities:** Critical infrastructure, such as power grids and water treatment systems, require robust security to prevent disruptions with widespread societal impact.

- **Manufacturing:** Industrial control systems (ICS) and supply chain networks are vulnerable to cyber-physical attacks that can halt production lines.

These scenarios require customized defense strategies that consider both technical and operational factors unique to each industry.

23.2 Core Components of Industry-Specific Cyber Defense

A tailored approach to industry-specific cybersecurity involves several key components that must be adapted to the particular challenges of each sector:

Customized Risk Assessments

- **Sector-Specific Threats:**
  Identify risks unique to your industry, such as medical

device vulnerabilities in healthcare or payment system breaches in retail.

- **Impact Analysis:**
  Evaluate not only financial and data losses but also potential harm to human life and public safety in critical sectors.

Regulatory and Compliance Alignment

- **Industry Regulations:**
  Ensure that security measures comply with sector-specific regulations (e.g., HIPAA for healthcare, PCI-DSS for finance, NERC CIP for energy).

- **Auditing and Reporting:**
  Implement regular compliance audits and transparent reporting practices to meet legal obligations and build trust with stakeholders.

Technology and Operational Integration

- **Operational Technology (OT) Security:**
  In industries like energy and manufacturing, integrate cybersecurity with physical controls and SCADA system protections.

- **Advanced Data Protection:**
  Tailor encryption, Data Loss Prevention (DLP), and backup strategies to the type and sensitivity of data handled in each industry.

- **Network Segmentation:**
  Isolate critical systems from general networks to contain breaches and minimize impact.

Incident Response and Recovery Tailored to Sector Needs

- **Sector-Specific Incident Plans:**
  Develop incident response plans that address the
  unique operational requirements and potential
  cascading effects in your industry.

- **Cross-Functional Coordination:**
  Involve both IT and operational teams (e.g., hospital
  administrators, factory managers) to ensure a
  coordinated response.

23.3 Implementing Industry-Specific Cyber Defense

Deploying industry-specific defenses requires a strategic,
multi-step approach:

Step 1: Conduct a Sector-Specific Risk Assessment

- **Identify Critical Assets:**
  List systems and data that are vital to your industry's
  operations.

- **Evaluate Unique Threats:**
  Consider both common cyber threats and those unique
  to your sector (e.g., ransomware in retail, supply chain
  attacks in manufacturing).

- **Prioritize Risks:**
  Use a risk matrix tailored to your industry to rank
  vulnerabilities based on potential impact and
  likelihood.

Step 2: Develop and Enforce Custom Security Policies

- **Policy Framework:**
  Create policies that address sector-specific challenges. For example, a healthcare policy might include strict controls on accessing patient records, while a retail policy could focus on securing POS systems.

- **Compliance Alignment:**
  Ensure policies meet industry regulations and are periodically reviewed to adapt to changing threats.

- **Training Programs:**
  Tailor training to address specific risks in your industry, incorporating real-world examples and case studies relevant to your sector.

Step 3: Deploy Tailored Security Technologies

- **For Healthcare:**
  Implement solutions such as secure Electronic Health Record (EHR) systems and device management for medical equipment.

- **For Finance:**
  Utilize robust encryption, secure payment processing systems, and fraud detection algorithms.

- **For Retail:**
  Protect e-commerce platforms and POS systems with application firewalls and transaction monitoring tools.

- **For Energy and Manufacturing:**
  Integrate specialized OT security measures with traditional IT controls, ensuring the resilience of SCADA and ICS systems.

- **Network Segmentation:**
  Apply segmentation and Zero Trust principles to isolate critical systems from general access across all sectors.

Step 4: Continuous Monitoring and Incident Preparedness

- **Real-Time Monitoring:**
  Deploy SIEM and industry-specific monitoring tools to continuously track system activity.

- **Incident Response Drills:**
  Conduct regular simulations and tabletop exercises tailored to the unique scenarios of your industry.

- **Feedback and Improvement:**
  Use lessons learned from drills and actual incidents to refine security measures and update policies.

Actionable Task

- **Industry Risk Inventory Exercise:**
  Develop a detailed inventory of critical assets and systems specific to your industry. Create a risk assessment matrix that categorizes these assets based on unique sector vulnerabilities. Identify one high-risk area and draft a remediation plan that includes specific controls, monitoring tools, and incident response strategies. Present your findings to relevant stakeholders for feedback.

- **Sector Policy Drafting Exercise:**
  Draft a sample security policy addressing a key area of concern in your industry—such as securing medical devices in healthcare or safeguarding payment systems in retail. Include detailed procedures, compliance requirements, and training guidelines. Circulate the

draft among internal teams (e.g., IT, operations, compliance) to refine and enhance the policy.

23.4 Real-World Applications and Case Studies

Case Study 1: Healthcare Cyber Defense

A large hospital network faced repeated cyber-attacks targeting patient records and medical devices:

- **Risk Assessment:**
  Conducted a comprehensive assessment focusing on the vulnerabilities of medical devices and EHR systems.

- **Policy and Technology:**
  Implemented robust encryption, strict access controls, and network segmentation to isolate critical systems.

- **Training and Awareness:**
  Regularly trained staff on the importance of secure data handling and recognizing phishing attacks.

- **Outcome:**
  The hospital network achieved a 55% reduction in security incidents and improved patient data protection, enhancing overall trust and regulatory compliance.

Case Study 2: Financial Services Cybersecurity

A multinational bank experienced targeted attacks aimed at its online banking platform:

- **Risk Assessment:**
  Identified vulnerabilities in its digital channels through rigorous testing and continuous monitoring.

- **Custom Solutions:**
  Deployed advanced encryption, multi-factor authentication (MFA), and fraud detection systems tailored to financial transactions.

- **Incident Response:**
  Implemented an incident response plan that integrated real-time monitoring and rapid remediation measures.

- **Outcome:**
  The bank reduced unauthorized access incidents by 50%, increased customer trust, and met stringent regulatory requirements.

Case Study 3: Securing Critical Infrastructure in Energy

A national energy provider needed to protect its control systems and critical infrastructure:

- **Integrated Risk Management:**
  Performed a thorough risk assessment that evaluated both IT and OT vulnerabilities.

- **Segmentation and Monitoring:**
  Segmented its network to isolate control systems and deployed specialized SCADA monitoring tools.

- **Incident Preparedness:**
  Developed and regularly tested an incident response plan that coordinated IT and operational teams.

- **Outcome:**
  The provider reduced the risk of cascading failures by 60% and ensured uninterrupted energy supply, safeguarding both operations and public safety.

Global Insight:
A European transportation authority implemented industry-specific cybersecurity measures that integrated IT and OT protections, resulting in a 50% reduction in service disruptions and setting a global benchmark for secure transportation systems.

23.5 Resources and Next Steps

To further your understanding and enhance your defenses in industry-specific environments, consider these resources:

- **Online Courses:**

    - Coursera, Udemy, and Cybrary offer courses tailored to specific industries, such as healthcare cybersecurity, financial services protection, and OT security for energy and manufacturing.

- **Books:**

    - *"Cybersecurity for Critical Infrastructure"*

    - *"Industry-Specific Cybersecurity: Strategies and Best Practices"*

- **Certifications:**

    - Consider certifications such as Certified Healthcare Information Security and Privacy Practitioner (HCISPP), Certified Financial Services Auditor (CFSA), or Global Industrial Cyber Security Professional (GICSP).

- **Professional Organizations:**

  - Engage with industry groups like the Healthcare Information and Management Systems Society (HIMSS), the Financial Services Information Sharing and Analysis Center (FS-ISAC), or the Industrial Internet Consortium (IIC) for networking and best practices.

- **Tools and Platforms:**

  - Experiment with sector-specific monitoring and risk management tools that support your industry's unique requirements.

- **Conferences and Workshops:**

  - Attend industry-specific cybersecurity conferences, such as the Healthcare Cybersecurity Conference or the Critical Infrastructure Protection Conference, to stay current on emerging trends and challenges.

Practical Tip:
Start by conducting an industry-specific risk assessment focused on your critical assets. Use the insights from this assessment to update your security policies and deploy targeted monitoring tools. Regularly review and refine your approach based on real-world feedback and emerging threats.

23.6 Chapter Takeaways

Key Points:

- **Industry-specific scenarios** highlight the unique cybersecurity challenges faced by different sectors, from healthcare and finance to energy and manufacturing.

- A tailored approach to cyber defense involves customized risk assessments, compliance with industry regulations, and integration of specialized technologies.

- Core components include **sector-specific risk management, regulatory alignment, technology integration, and continuous monitoring.**

- Real-world case studies demonstrate significant improvements—often reducing security incidents by 50–60%—when tailored security measures are implemented.

- Continuous training, stakeholder engagement, and proactive adaptation to industry trends are essential for maintaining a resilient security posture.

23.7 Test Your Knowledge

1. **Which of the following is a key reason for implementing industry-specific cybersecurity measures?**
   A. To generalize security controls for all sectors
   B. To address the unique operational and regulatory challenges of different industries
   C. To reduce the number of security policies

D. To eliminate the need for third-party risk assessments

2. **What is one primary benefit of network segmentation in critical infrastructure sectors like energy and manufacturing?**
A. It increases the number of connected devices
B. It restricts lateral movement, isolating critical systems from general network traffic
C. It simplifies regulatory compliance
D. It enhances Wi-Fi signal strength

3. **Scenario Question:**
Imagine you are the cybersecurity manager for a multinational healthcare organization. Describe one strategy you would implement to secure sensitive patient data and medical devices and explain how you would measure its effectiveness. Include specific tools or methodologies in your answer.

4. **Reflective Exercise:**
Draw a simplified diagram of your organization's network architecture specific to your industry (e.g., a retail POS system or a manufacturing control network). Identify key assets and potential vulnerabilities, then propose one mitigation strategy for each. Outline how you would update your security policies and communicate these changes to both technical staff and senior management.

23.8 Final Thoughts

Industry-specific cybersecurity scenarios underscore the need for tailored defense strategies that account for the unique challenges of different sectors. Whether you are protecting patient data in healthcare, securing financial transactions, or safeguarding critical infrastructure in energy and manufacturing, the principles of risk management, regulatory compliance, and continuous monitoring remain paramount. This chapter has provided a detailed exploration of the strategies, technologies, and best practices that form the backbone of industry-specific cyber defense, reinforced by real-world case studies and actionable tasks.

As you continue your journey through this book, remember that the effectiveness of your cybersecurity efforts depends on adapting general principles to meet the distinct needs of your industry. By continuously refining your approaches and engaging with sector-specific resources, you can build a resilient defense that not only meets regulatory requirements but also enhances operational continuity and stakeholder trust.

Thank you for exploring Chapter 23. Apply these insights and exercises to develop a customized cybersecurity strategy for your industry and continue your journey toward mastering cyber defense.

End of Chapter 23

Part 6: Building a Career in Cyber Defense

Chapter 24: Cybersecurity Career Paths

Cybersecurity is a dynamic and rapidly evolving field that offers diverse career opportunities. Whether you're a newcomer looking to break into the industry or an experienced IT professional seeking to specialize, understanding the various roles, required skills, and growth trajectories is essential. In this chapter, we explore the spectrum of career paths in cyber defense—from technical positions like penetration testers and SOC analysts to strategic roles such as CISOs and risk managers. We also provide actionable tasks, real-world case studies, and resource recommendations to help you navigate your career journey in cybersecurity.

Expert Insight:
"Cybersecurity careers are as diverse as the threats we face. The key is to identify your strengths and interests, then build the skills and certifications needed to excel in your chosen path." — Cybersecurity Career Advisor

---

24.1 What Are Cybersecurity Career Paths?

Cybersecurity career paths encompass a range of roles that protect organizations against cyber threats. These roles can be broadly categorized into technical, analytical, managerial, and consulting functions. Each role requires a unique blend of technical expertise, soft skills, and, often, specialized certifications. Understanding these paths is crucial for aligning your career goals with the demands of the industry.

Key objectives in exploring cybersecurity career paths include:

- **Identifying Roles:** Understanding the spectrum of positions available—from entry-level roles to executive positions.

- **Skill Requirements:** Knowing the technical, analytical, and interpersonal skills needed for each role.

- **Certifications and Education:** Recognizing the importance of formal education, certifications, and continuous learning.

- **Career Growth:** Mapping out potential career trajectories and opportunities for advancement.

24.2 Core Cybersecurity Roles

Security Operations Center (SOC) Analyst

- **Role:**
  Monitors network traffic, analyzes security alerts, and responds to incidents.

- **Key Skills:**
  Proficiency with SIEM tools, basic networking, threat analysis, and incident response.

- **Certifications:**
  CompTIA Security+, Certified SOC Analyst (CSA).

Penetration Tester (Ethical Hacker)

- **Role:**
  Simulates attacks on systems to identify vulnerabilities before malicious hackers can exploit them.

- **Key Skills:**
  Programming, understanding of networks and operating systems, knowledge of tools like Metasploit and Burp Suite.

- **Certifications:**
  Certified Ethical Hacker (CEH), Offensive Security Certified Professional (OSCP).

Threat Intelligence Analyst

- **Role:**
  Analyzes threat data to identify trends, adversary tactics, and emerging risks.

- **Key Skills:**
  Research, data analysis, familiarity with threat intelligence platforms, and strong communication.

- **Certifications:**
  Certified Threat Intelligence Analyst (CTIA), GIAC Cyber Threat Intelligence (GCTI).

Digital Forensics Expert

- **Role:**
  Investigates cybercrimes by collecting, analyzing, and preserving digital evidence.

- **Key Skills:**
  Forensic tools (e.g., EnCase, FTK), attention to detail, knowledge of legal procedures.

- **Certifications:**
  Certified Computer Forensics Examiner (CCFE), GIAC Certified Forensic Analyst (GCFA).

Cybersecurity Consultant

- **Role:**
  Advises organizations on security best practices, risk management, and technology implementation.

- **Key Skills:**
  Broad technical knowledge, risk assessment, project management, and excellent communication.

- **Certifications:**
  CISSP, Certified Information Security Manager (CISM).

Chief Information Security Officer (CISO)

- **Role:**
  Sets the strategic direction for an organization's cybersecurity initiatives and ensures alignment with business objectives.

- **Key Skills:**
  Leadership, strategic planning, risk management, regulatory compliance, and excellent communication.

- **Certifications:**
  CISSP, CISM, and executive-level training programs.

24.3 Developing Your Cybersecurity Career

Embarking on a cybersecurity career involves planning, education, and continuous skill development. Here's a step-by-step guide to help you build your career path:

Step 1: Self-Assessment and Goal Setting

- **Identify Your Strengths and Interests:**
  Reflect on your skills, interests, and career aspirations. Are you more inclined toward technical roles like penetration testing, or do you prefer strategic planning as a CISO?

- **Set Clear Goals:**
  Define short-term and long-term career objectives. Establish milestones such as earning a specific certification or transitioning to a new role.

Step 2: Education and Skill Development

- **Formal Education:**
  Pursue degrees in computer science, information technology, or cybersecurity. Consider specialized programs that focus on security.

- **Certifications:**
  Research and obtain relevant certifications that align with your desired career path. Certifications validate your skills and increase your marketability.

- **Hands-On Experience:**
  Engage in practical exercises, internships, or lab environments. Participate in Capture The Flag (CTF) competitions and contribute to open-source projects.

Step 3: Build a Professional Network

- **Industry Events:**
  Attend cybersecurity conferences, workshops, and webinars to connect with professionals and stay updated on industry trends.

- **Online Communities:**
  Join forums, social media groups, and professional organizations like (ISC)^2, ISACA, or local cybersecurity meetups.

- **Mentorship:**
  Seek mentors who can provide guidance, share experiences, and help navigate your career path.

Step 4: Gain Real-World Experience

- **Entry-Level Roles:**
  Start in roles such as SOC Analyst, junior penetration tester, or IT security specialist to gain foundational experience.

- **Internships and Projects:**
  Work on real-world projects, internships, or freelance assignments to build your portfolio.

- **Specialization:**
  As you gain experience, consider specializing in areas like threat intelligence, digital forensics, or cloud security based on industry demands and your interests.

Step 5: Continuous Learning and Adaptation

- **Stay Current:**
  Cybersecurity is a rapidly evolving field. Keep up with emerging threats, new technologies, and evolving best practices.

- **Advanced Training:**
  Pursue advanced certifications, attend workshops, and consider further education (e.g., a master's degree in cybersecurity) to stay ahead.

- **Feedback and Reflection:**
  Regularly assess your progress and seek feedback from peers and mentors. Adapt your goals as the industry evolves.

Actionable Task

- **Career Roadmap Exercise:**
  Create a personalized cybersecurity career roadmap. List your current skills, identify gaps, and set specific short-term and long-term goals. Include milestones such as obtaining certifications, gaining experience in specific roles, and networking targets. Share your roadmap with a mentor or peer group for feedback and adjust it based on their input.

- **Portfolio Development:**
  Identify at least two projects or practical exercises (e.g., a penetration test report, a threat intelligence analysis) to include in your professional portfolio. Document your methodologies, findings, and outcomes, and consider publishing your work on a personal blog or professional networking site.

24.4 Real-World Applications and Case Studies

Case Study 1: Transitioning from IT to Cyber Defense

An IT professional with a background in network administration transitioned into a cybersecurity career by:

- **Skill Enhancement:**
  Pursuing certifications like CompTIA Security+ and CEH.

- **Hands-On Experience:**
  Participating in CTF competitions and completing penetration testing projects.

- **Networking and Mentorship:**
  Engaging with cybersecurity forums and attending local meetups.

- **Outcome:**
  Within two years, the professional advanced to a SOC Analyst role and later specialized in threat intelligence, demonstrating that targeted learning and networking can facilitate a successful career transition.

Case Study 2: Climbing the Cybersecurity Ladder in Financial Services

A cybersecurity consultant in the financial services sector leveraged her expertise to build a diversified career:

- **Starting Point:**
  The consultant began as a penetration tester, gaining hands-on experience with vulnerabilities in financial systems.

- **Skill Diversification:**
  She earned additional certifications (CISSP, CISM) and expanded her skills to include risk management and governance.

- **Leadership Transition:**
  Her comprehensive expertise enabled her to advance to a cybersecurity management role, eventually serving as the head of security for a major financial institution.

- **Outcome:**
  Her career trajectory illustrates the value of continuous learning, specialization, and strategic networking in advancing within the cybersecurity field.

Global Insight:

A European technology firm established an internal mentorship program and sponsored continuous education for its cybersecurity staff. This initiative resulted in a 40% increase in internal promotions and a significant boost in overall team competency and innovation.

24.5 Resources and Next Steps

To further your career in cybersecurity, explore these resources:

- **Online Courses:**
  - Platforms like Coursera, Udemy, and Cybrary offer courses on various cybersecurity domains, from basic security fundamentals to advanced threat intelligence.

- **Books:**
  - *"Cybersecurity Career Guide"*
  - *"The Hacker Playbook"* series for hands-on technical insights.

- **Certifications:**
  - Consider entry-level certifications such as CompTIA Security+ for beginners, and advanced

certifications like CISSP, CEH, or OSCP as you progress.

- **Professional Organizations:**

  o Engage with $(ISC)^2$, ISACA, and local cybersecurity associations for networking, mentorship, and career opportunities.

- **Conferences and Workshops:**

  o Attend events such as DEF CON, Black Hat, RSA Conference, and regional cybersecurity meetups to gain insights and connect with industry professionals.

- **Career Portals and Forums:**

  o Explore platforms like LinkedIn, CyberSecJobs, and Reddit's r/cybersecurity for job listings, career advice, and networking opportunities.

Practical Tip:
Start by setting specific career goals and mapping out your learning path. Identify the certifications and skills most relevant to your desired role and actively engage with industry communities to gain insights and mentorship.

24.6 Chapter Takeaways

Key Points:

- **Cybersecurity career paths** are diverse, ranging from technical roles like SOC Analysts and penetration testers to strategic positions such as CISOs and cybersecurity consultants.

- Understanding your strengths and interests is essential for choosing the right path, and continuous learning through certifications and hands-on projects is key to advancement.

- Building a professional network, participating in industry events, and engaging in mentorship are critical for career growth.

- Real-world case studies demonstrate that targeted skill development, certification, and networking can facilitate successful career transitions and progression.

- A proactive career roadmap, combined with ongoing education and networking, is crucial to mastering the evolving field of cybersecurity.

24.7 Test Your Knowledge

1. **Which of the following roles is primarily responsible for monitoring network traffic and responding to security incidents?**
   A. Penetration Tester
   B. SOC Analyst
   C. Cybersecurity Consultant
   D. Chief Information Security Officer

2. **What is one key benefit of obtaining certifications in cybersecurity?**
   A. They guarantee a job immediately
   B. They validate your skills and increase your marketability
   C. They replace the need for practical experience
   D. They simplify technical tasks

3. **Scenario Question:**
   Imagine you are an IT professional seeking to transition into cybersecurity. Describe one specific certification or training program you would pursue and explain how it would help you develop the skills required for a role such as a penetration tester or SOC analyst. Include how you would integrate hands-on experience into your learning process.

4. **Reflective Exercise:**
   Create a personal career roadmap that outlines your short-term and long-term goals in cybersecurity. Identify at least three key milestones (e.g., obtaining a certification, gaining a specific job role, attending industry conferences) and explain how you plan to achieve each. Discuss how you would document your progress and adjust your roadmap based on industry trends and personal growth.

24.8 Final Thoughts

Building a successful career in cybersecurity requires a blend of technical expertise, continuous learning, and proactive networking. This chapter has provided a comprehensive overview of the diverse career paths available in cyber defense, detailed the skills and certifications needed for various roles, and offered practical guidance for mapping out your professional journey. Whether you aspire to become a SOC analyst, penetration tester, threat intelligence specialist, or even a CISO, a clear understanding of these pathways will help you navigate the complexities of the industry.

As you continue your journey through this book, remember that the key to success in cybersecurity is continuous improvement and staying ahead of emerging threats. Your career growth will be shaped by the skills you acquire, the certifications you earn, and the network you build along the way.

Thank you for exploring Chapter 24. Apply these insights and actionable tasks to map out your cybersecurity career and continue your journey toward mastering cyber defense and achieving professional success.

End of Chapter 24

The future of cybersecurity is a dynamic landscape shaped by rapid technological advancements, evolving threats, and global interconnectedness. As we look ahead, emerging technologies such as artificial intelligence, quantum computing, and the expansion of IoT and cloud services will continue to redefine the cyber defense paradigm. In this chapter, we explore key trends, innovative strategies, and the challenges that will shape cybersecurity in the coming years. Drawing on insights from previous chapters and expert analysis, you will learn how to anticipate future risks, adapt your defense strategies, and position yourself for success in an ever-evolving field.

Expert Insight:
"The future of cybersecurity is not a distant possibility—it's already here. Organizations must embrace emerging technologies and continuously adapt their strategies to stay ahead of increasingly sophisticated threats." — Cybersecurity Futurist

25.1 What Is the Future of Cybersecurity?

The future of cybersecurity involves the integration of new technologies and methodologies to address both current and emerging threats. It encompasses:

- **Proactive Defense:** Moving from reactive incident response to proactive threat prevention and risk mitigation.

- **Integration of Emerging Technologies:** Leveraging advancements in AI, quantum computing, and IoT security to bolster defenses.

- **Holistic and Adaptive Strategies:** Combining technical, operational, and human-centric approaches for comprehensive security.

- **Global Collaboration:** Enhancing international cooperation and information sharing to combat transnational cyber threats.

- **Regulatory Evolution:** Adapting to new legal and ethical standards as digital ecosystems grow more complex.

These trends highlight the shift toward a more anticipatory and resilient cybersecurity posture, where continuous learning and innovation are essential.

25.2 Core Trends and Emerging Technologies

Artificial Intelligence and Machine Learning

- **Enhanced Threat Detection:**
  AI and ML are increasingly used to analyze vast datasets and detect subtle anomalies, enabling quicker identification of emerging threats.

- **Automated Response:**
  Machine learning algorithms can automate routine responses, reducing the time to mitigate incidents.

- **Adaptive Security:**
  Continuous learning models adapt to new attack patterns, making defenses more resilient over time.

Quantum Computing and Post-Quantum Cryptography

- **Quantum Threats:**
  Quantum computing poses a significant risk to traditional cryptographic algorithms such as RSA and ECC.

- **Transition to PQC:**
  Post-Quantum Cryptography aims to develop new encryption methods that are secure against quantum attacks, ensuring long-term data protection.

IoT, OT, and Cloud Security

- **Expanding Attack Surface:**
  The proliferation of IoT and OT devices increases the number of potential entry points for cyber-attacks.

- **Integrated Security Solutions:**
  Future strategies will require seamless integration of IT, IoT, OT, and cloud security measures to protect a hybrid environment.

- **Edge Computing:**
  With more processing happening at the network edge, securing decentralized systems becomes paramount.

Zero Trust Architecture

- **Eliminating Implicit Trust:**
  Zero Trust models require continuous verification of every access request, regardless of location, to minimize lateral movement.

- **Micro-Segmentation:**
  Dividing networks into smaller, isolated segments
  further strengthens defenses against internal threats.

Blockchain and Distributed Ledger Technologies

- **Data Integrity and Transparency:**
  Blockchain can enhance data integrity and provide
  immutable audit trails, reducing fraud and ensuring
  compliance.

- **Decentralized Security:**
  Distributed ledger technologies offer new paradigms
  for secure identity management and transactional
  security.

5G and Beyond

- **Increased Connectivity:**
  The rollout of 5G networks will accelerate data
  transmission and connectivity, creating both
  opportunities and challenges for cybersecurity.

- **Enhanced Attack Vectors:**
  Faster, more connected networks will require
  advanced security measures to protect against high-
  speed, sophisticated attacks.

25.3 Implementing Future Cybersecurity Strategies

Adapting to the future of cybersecurity requires a proactive,
multi-layered approach that integrates emerging technologies
and anticipates new threats.

Step 1: Conduct a Forward-Looking Risk Assessment

- **Identify Emerging Threats:**
  Use threat intelligence to predict future attack vectors and assess the potential impact of emerging technologies on your security posture.

- **Evaluate Current Defenses:**
  Assess the robustness of your existing security controls against new types of attacks, such as quantum-enabled breaches.

- **Prioritize Investments:**
  Allocate resources to areas with the greatest potential impact, such as upgrading encryption methods or enhancing zero trust frameworks.

Step 2: Integrate Emerging Technologies

- **AI and ML Integration:**
  Enhance your threat detection systems with AI and ML algorithms that adapt to new data and learn from evolving attack patterns.

- **PQC Transition Planning:**
  Begin pilot projects for post-quantum cryptographic solutions, testing their performance and compatibility with existing systems.

- **Expand IoT and OT Security:**
  Implement advanced monitoring and segmentation for IoT and OT environments, ensuring that these devices are not the weak link in your network.

Step 3: Revise Policies and Governance Frameworks

- **Update Security Policies:**
  Revise your cybersecurity policies to incorporate emerging technologies and address new threat landscapes. Include provisions for quantum-resistant encryption and zero trust principles.

- **Enhance Governance:**
  Strengthen governance structures to ensure that strategic decisions align with the rapidly evolving cybersecurity environment.

- **Continuous Learning:**
  Establish continuous improvement processes that incorporate lessons from new technologies and threat intelligence.

Step 4: Foster Global Collaboration

- **Information Sharing:**
  Participate in international threat intelligence sharing communities to stay informed about global cyber trends.

- **Collaborative Research:**
  Engage with academic institutions, industry consortia, and government agencies to contribute to the development of next-generation security solutions.

- **Policy Advocacy:**
  Work with regulatory bodies to shape emerging standards and frameworks that address the challenges of a hyper-connected world.

Step 5: Continuous Monitoring and Adaptation

- **Real-Time Analytics:**
  Invest in SIEM and SOAR platforms enhanced with AI/ML capabilities to continuously monitor your digital environment.

- **Adaptive Response:**
  Ensure your incident response plans are flexible and regularly updated to incorporate emerging threats and technologies.

- **Feedback Mechanism:**
  Create feedback loops to review the effectiveness of new security measures and adjust strategies based on real-world performance.

Actionable Task

- **Future-Readiness Assessment:**
  Conduct a comprehensive review of your current cybersecurity posture with a focus on emerging threats such as quantum computing and advanced AI-driven attacks. Develop a risk assessment matrix that identifies potential vulnerabilities in the context of future technologies. Draft a plan outlining specific action—such as piloting a PQC algorithm or enhancing your AI-based threat detection system—and present this plan to your leadership team for feedback.

- **Technology Integration Exercise:**
  Choose an emerging technology, such as zero trust or blockchain-based identity management, and create a pilot project to test its feasibility within your organization. Document the process, measure performance metrics (e.g., detection accuracy, response

times), and prepare a report with recommendations for broader implementation.

25.4 Real-World Applications and Case Studies

Case Study 1: AI-Driven Threat Detection in a Global Bank

A multinational bank integrated AI and ML into its cybersecurity operations:

- **Data Aggregation:**
  The bank consolidated logs from various sources using an advanced SIEM enhanced with machine learning.

- **Predictive Analysis:**
  AI models were trained on historical attack data to predict and flag anomalies.

- **Automated Response:**
  Integration with a SOAR platform enabled automated containment measures.

- **Outcome:**
  The bank achieved a 40% improvement in threat detection accuracy and reduced its Mean Time to Respond (MTTR) by 35%, positioning it to counter increasingly sophisticated cyber-attacks.

Case Study 2: Preparing for Quantum Threats in Critical Infrastructure

A European energy company initiated a pilot project to transition from classical cryptography to post-quantum algorithms:

- **Risk Assessment:**
  The company identified its RSA-based systems as vulnerable to quantum attacks.

- **PQC Pilot:**
  A lattice-based encryption algorithm was implemented in a controlled environment, demonstrating strong performance with minimal latency.

- **Outcome:**
  The pilot project informed a phased migration plan, reducing the company's long-term risk profile and ensuring readiness for future regulatory requirements related to quantum security.

Case Study 3: IoT and Zero Trust Integration in a Smart City

A smart city project deployed a Zero Trust model across its IoT networks:

- **Security Architecture:**
  The project segmented its IoT devices and implemented continuous authentication protocols.

- **Monitoring and Analytics:**
  AI-driven analytics monitored device behavior, quickly detecting anomalies.

- **Outcome:**
  The initiative resulted in a 50% reduction in unauthorized access incidents and significantly enhanced the overall security and resilience of the city's digital infrastructure.

Global Insight:
A leading Asian conglomerate integrated multiple emerging

technologies—AI, blockchain, and post-quantum cryptography—into its cyber defense framework, achieving a 45% improvement in overall security posture and setting a benchmark for the industry.

25.5 Resources and Next Steps

To further prepare for the future of cybersecurity, consider the following resources:

- **Online Courses:**

  - Coursera, Udemy, and Cybrary offer courses on emerging technologies such as quantum computing, AI in cybersecurity, and zero trust architectures.

- **Books:**

  - *"Quantum Computing for Everyone"*

  - *"Machine Learning and Security: Protecting Systems with Data and Algorithms"*

- **Certifications:**

  - Explore emerging certifications focused on AI and quantum security, such as the Certified Quantum Security Practitioner (CQSP) (if available) or advanced courses in cybersecurity analytics.

- **Professional Organizations:**

  - Engage with IEEE, ISACA, and the Cloud Security Alliance (CSA) for research, webinars, and networking on future cybersecurity trends.

- **Tools and Platforms:**

  - Experiment with open-source frameworks such as TensorFlow for AI and simulate quantum-resistant algorithms using platforms provided by NIST.

- **Conferences and Workshops:**

  - Attend events like the RSA Conference, Black Hat, and emerging quantum computing summits to stay ahead of new developments.

Practical Tip:
Set up a pilot project in your lab to test the performance of an AI-driven threat detection model or a post-quantum encryption algorithm. Document your findings, compare them with existing systems, and use this data to plan a gradual integration of new technologies into your production environment.

25.6 Chapter Takeaways

Key Points:

- **The future of cybersecurity** is shaped by emerging technologies such as AI, quantum computing, IoT, and blockchain, which are set to revolutionize threat detection and response.

- **Proactive defense** is critical: transitioning from reactive measures to predictive, adaptive strategies ensures robust protection.

- Core trends include **AI-driven analytics, post-quantum cryptography, Zero Trust architectures,** and enhanced global collaboration.

- Implementing future-ready strategies involves conducting forward-looking risk assessments, integrating emerging technologies into existing frameworks, and continuously monitoring for new threats.

- Real-world case studies demonstrate tangible benefits, such as significant improvements in threat detection accuracy and reduced response times.

- Continuous adaptation, training, and collaboration are essential to keep pace with the rapidly evolving cybersecurity landscape.

25.7 Test Your Knowledge

1. **Which of the following best describes a primary benefit of integrating AI and machine learning into cybersecurity?**
   A. They eliminate the need for human analysts.
   B. They enable rapid detection of anomalies by processing large datasets.
   C. They replace traditional encryption methods entirely.
   D. They guarantee zero false positives.

2. **What is the primary goal of post-quantum cryptography (PQC)?**
   A. To improve the speed of encryption algorithms.
   B. To develop cryptographic methods resistant to quantum computing attacks.
   C. To simplify key management processes.
   D. To integrate blockchain into security protocols.

3. **Scenario Question:**
   Imagine you are a cybersecurity architect tasked with preparing your organization for future quantum threats. Describe one PQC algorithm you would consider and explain how you would pilot its implementation. Include specific steps, tools, or performance metrics to assess its viability.

4. **Reflective Exercise:**
   Draw a simplified diagram of a future-proof cybersecurity architecture that incorporates AI-driven threat detection and post-quantum cryptographic solutions. Identify one potential challenge in integrating these technologies, propose a mitigation strategy, and outline how you would communicate these changes to your security team.

25.8 Final Thoughts

The future of cybersecurity is a dynamic frontier where emerging technologies and evolving threats intersect. As we prepare for a new era marked by AI, quantum computing, and increasingly interconnected digital ecosystems, proactive and adaptive defense strategies become paramount. This chapter has explored key trends, innovative strategies, and real-world case studies that highlight the transformative potential of advanced technologies in securing digital assets.

By embracing continuous learning, leveraging cutting-edge tools, and fostering global collaboration, organizations can build a resilient cybersecurity framework that anticipates and neutralizes threats before they materialize. The insights and actionable tasks provided in this chapter will serve as a roadmap to help you navigate the challenges of tomorrow's cyber landscape.

Thank you for exploring Chapter 25. Apply these insights to evolve your cybersecurity strategy and stay ahead of emerging threats as you continue your journey toward mastering cyber defense in an ever-changing world.

End of Chapter 25

Conclusion

Mastering Cyber Defense in a Dynamic World

As we reach the end of this comprehensive guide, it's clear that the field of cybersecurity is both challenging and exhilarating. Throughout this book, we have explored the multifaceted nature of cyber defense—from foundational principles and frameworks to advanced topics and real-world case studies. The journey through risk management, network security, endpoint protection, identity and access management, data protection, and beyond has illuminated not only the technical intricacies of defending digital assets but also the strategic, ethical, and human-centric dimensions that shape effective cyber defense.

Final Expert Insight:
"Cyber defense is a continuous journey. The insights and strategies you've learned here are not endpoints but foundations on which you must build, adapt, and innovate as threats evolve." — Cybersecurity Strategist

---

Summary of Key Insights

- **Foundational Principles:**
  We began with the fundamentals of cybersecurity—understanding the CIA triad, defense in depth, and risk management. These principles establish the framework for all subsequent security measures and remind us that protection is a layered, continuous process.

- **Structured Frameworks and Compliance:**
  Chapters on cybersecurity frameworks, standards, and governance underscored the importance of having structured, policy-driven approaches to manage risk. Whether it's aligning with international standards like NIST or ISO 27001 or navigating complex regulatory environments such as GDPR or HIPAA, a strong governance model is essential for maintaining resilience.

- **Technical Defenses:**
  Through detailed explorations of network, endpoint, application, and cloud security, we learned how to deploy and integrate technologies that safeguard digital infrastructures. Each technical control—from firewalls and SIEM systems to encryption and Zero Trust architectures—plays a critical role in defending against a rapidly evolving threat landscape.

- **Offensive Security and Threat Intelligence:**
  The proactive approaches of offensive security and cyber threat intelligence empower organizations to think like adversaries, thereby identifying vulnerabilities before they can be exploited. Real-world case studies from high-profile cyber-attacks have shown the value of learning from incidents and continuously refining security strategies.

- **Human-Centric Defense:**
  Recognizing that technology alone cannot secure an organization, we emphasized the importance of security awareness, training, and a culture of vigilance. Empowering employees through education transforms every individual into a critical line of defense, reinforcing the technical measures in place.

320

- **Future Trends and Innovation:**
  As emerging technologies such as AI, quantum computing, and IoT reshape the cyber landscape, our final chapters have provided a glimpse into the future of cybersecurity. Proactive adaptation, continuous learning, and global collaboration will be essential in navigating these uncharted territories.

Future Directions and Continuous Improvement

The field of cybersecurity is in a constant state of evolution. New threats emerge, technologies advance, and regulatory landscapes shift. Here are some key future directions to consider:

- **Embrace Emerging Technologies:**
  Stay ahead by integrating AI and machine learning into threat detection, transitioning to post-quantum cryptography, and securing increasingly connected IoT environments. These technologies promise to revolutionize how we predict, detect, and respond to cyber threats.

- **Foster a Culture of Continuous Learning:**
  Cybersecurity is a dynamic discipline. Regular training, simulated exercises, and industry certifications are vital to keep pace with new developments. Establish feedback loops to incorporate lessons from incidents and adapt your strategies accordingly.

- **Enhance Collaboration and Information Sharing:**
  No organization operates in isolation. Global cooperation, participation in information-sharing communities, and collaboration with industry and

government bodies can enhance your threat intelligence and fortify your defenses.

- **Invest in Robust Governance:**
  As threats become more complex, strengthening governance frameworks to align security practices with business objectives will remain a top priority. Ensure that leadership is engaged, policies are continuously updated, and compliance is rigorously maintained.

Call to Action

Your journey into cybersecurity doesn't end here—it's only the beginning. Take the following steps to build on the knowledge and strategies presented in this book:

1. **Review and Reflect:**
   Revisit key chapters and reflect on the foundational principles and advanced strategies. Consider how they apply to your organization or career aspirations.

2. **Implement and Innovate:**
   Identify one area in your current security posture that could benefit from improvement. Develop a plan to implement the strategies discussed and measure your progress with clear metrics.

3. **Stay Informed:**
   Cybersecurity is rapidly evolving. Commit to continuous learning through courses, certifications, and engagement with professional communities.

4. **Collaborate and Share:**
   Share your insights and experiences with peers and

mentors. Collaboration is key to staying ahead in the ever-changing landscape of cyber defense.

5. **Adapt to the Future:**
   Embrace emerging technologies and be proactive in updating your defenses. The future of cybersecurity is built on innovation and the willingness to adapt.

Final Thoughts

The journey to mastering cyber defense is ongoing and demands a balanced approach—one that integrates technical expertise, strategic planning, and a deep commitment to continuous improvement. By understanding and applying the insights shared in this book, you are well-equipped to face today's challenges and prepare for tomorrow's threats.

Cyber defense is not just a set of practices—it's a mindset, a culture, and a relentless pursuit of excellence in the face of evolving adversaries. As you move forward, let these principles guide your actions, inspire innovation, and empower you to build a secure and resilient digital future.

Thank you for joining us on this journey. Your proactive approach to cybersecurity will not only protect your organization but also contribute to a safer digital world for everyone.

End of Conclusion

Appendices

The following appendices provide additional resources, tools, and reference materials to support the concepts discussed throughout the book. They are designed to help you deepen your understanding, implement practical solutions, and serve as a quick reference guide as you continue your journey in cyber defense.

Appendix A: Glossary of Key Terms

This glossary defines the technical and industry-specific terms used throughout the book. Refer to it whenever you encounter unfamiliar terminology.

- **Access Control:**
  Policies and mechanisms that restrict access to digital resources, ensuring that only authorized users can perform specific actions.

- **Annualized Loss Expectancy (ALE):**
  A quantitative measure used to estimate the expected monetary loss for an asset due to a risk over a one-year period.

- **CIA Triad:**
  A fundamental model in cybersecurity representing Confidentiality, Integrity, and Availability.

- **Cyber Threat Intelligence (CTI):**
  The process of collecting, analyzing, and disseminating

information about potential cyber threats to inform proactive defense measures.

- **Defense in Depth:**
  A layered security strategy that employs multiple, independent security controls to protect digital assets.

- **Endpoint Detection and Response (EDR):**
  Solutions that continuously monitor and analyze endpoint activities to detect and respond to threats.

- **Identity and Access Management (IAM):**
  The policies, processes, and technologies used to manage digital identities and control user access to resources.

- **Incident Response (IR):**
  The structured approach for handling and mitigating security incidents, including detection, containment, eradication, and recovery.

- **Internet of Things (IoT):**
  The network of physical devices, vehicles, appliances, and other items embedded with sensors, software, and connectivity, enabling data exchange.

- **Operational Technology (OT):**
  Hardware and software that control physical devices, processes, and events in industrial environments.

- **Post-Quantum Cryptography (PQC):**
  Cryptographic algorithms designed to be secure against the potential threats posed by quantum computing.

- **Risk Management:**
  The process of identifying, assessing, and mitigating risks to an organization's assets and operations.

- **SIEM (Security Information and Event Management):**
  A system that aggregates and analyzes security-related data from multiple sources to detect, respond to, and report on incidents.

- **Zero Trust Architecture:**
  A security model that assumes no implicit trust—every access request must be continuously verified regardless of location.

Appendix B: Tools and Resources

A wide range of tools and platforms can assist you in implementing the strategies discussed in this book. Below is a curated list of essential tools and resource categories:

Security Tools

- **SIEM Platforms:**
  Splunk, IBM QRadar, and ELK Stack for log aggregation and real-time monitoring.

- **Endpoint Protection:**
  CrowdStrike, SentinelOne, and Carbon Black for advanced endpoint detection and response.

- **Penetration Testing Tools:**
  Metasploit, Burp Suite, Nmap, and OWASP ZAP for ethical hacking and vulnerability assessments.

- **Threat Intelligence Platforms:**
  MISP (Malware Information Sharing Platform), Recorded Future, and Anomali for aggregating and analyzing threat data.

- **Cloud Security Tools:**
  AWS Security Hub, Azure Security Center, and Google Cloud's Security Command Center for managing cloud and hybrid environments.

Governance and Compliance Platforms

- **GRC Solutions:**
  RSA Archer, MetricStream, and ServiceNow for managing governance, risk, and compliance processes.

- **Vulnerability Management Tools:**
  Nessus, Qualys, and OpenVAS for continuous vulnerability scanning and risk assessments.

Learning and Community Resources

- **Online Training Platforms:**
  Coursera, Udemy, Cybrary, and Pluralsight offer courses on cybersecurity fundamentals and advanced topics.

- **Professional Organizations:**
  (ISC)^2, ISACA, EC-Council, and (ISC)^2 provide certifications, networking opportunities, and industry insights.

- **Industry Forums and Blogs:**
  Follow sources like Krebs on Security, Dark Reading, and the SANS Institute for up-to-date research and news.s

These templates and checklists are designed to help you implement the frameworks and practices discussed in the book.

Incident Response Plan Template

- **Introduction:** Overview of the plan and its objectives.

- **Team Structure:** Roles and responsibilities of the incident response team.

- **Incident Classification:** Criteria for categorizing incident severity.

- **Response Procedures:** Detailed steps for detection, containment, eradication, and recovery.

- **Communication Protocols:** Internal and external communication strategies.

- **Post-Incident Review:** Procedures for conducting a lessons-learned session and updating policies.

Risk Assessment Matrix Template

- **Asset Inventory:** List of critical assets.

- **Threat Identification:** Potential threats for each asset.

- **Vulnerability Assessment:** Likelihood and impact ratings.

- **Risk Prioritization:** A matrix categorizing risks as high, medium, or low.

- **Mitigation Strategies:** Recommended actions to address each risk.

Vendor Risk Assessment Checklist

- **Vendor Profile:** Name, service provided, data access level.

- **Security Practices:** Evaluation of vendor's security policies, certifications, and audit reports.

- **Risk Scoring:** Assign a risk rating based on impact and likelihood.

- **Remediation Requirements:** Specific actions required for risk mitigation.

- **Review Schedule:** Timeline for periodic reassessments.

Appendix D: Further Reading and References

This section provides a list of recommended books, articles, and research papers that offer additional insights into the topics covered in this book.

Recommended Books

- *"Hacking: The Art of Exploitation"* by Jon Erickson

- *"The Web Application Hacker's Handbook"* by Dafydd Stuttard and Marcus Pinto

- *"Security Engineering: A Guide to Building Dependable Distributed Systems"* by Ross Anderson

- *"Quantum Computing for Computer Scientists"* by Noson S. Yanofsky and Mirco A. Mannucci

Key Articles and Research Papers

- "The NIST Cybersecurity Framework: A Comprehensive Guide" – NIST Special Publication 800-53

- "Post-Quantum Cryptography: Current State and Future Directions" – Journal of Cryptographic Engineering

- "Zero Trust Architecture: Principles and Implementation" – IEEE Security & Privacy Magazine

- "Threat Intelligence: Transforming Data into Actionable Insights" – SANS Institute Whitepapers

---

Final Note

These appendices are designed to serve as a practical companion to the main content of this book. They provide quick references, templates, and additional resources that can be used to implement and refine your cybersecurity strategies. Use them as a toolkit to support your ongoing learning and application of the principles discussed throughout the book.

End of Appendices

www.ingramcontent.com/pod-product-compliance
Lightning Source LLC
LaVergne TN
LVHW051430050326
832903LV00030BD/3014